MICHIGAN
SCOUNDRELS

MICHIGAN SCOUNDRELS

ROGUES, RASCALS AND RAPSCALLIONS

NORMA LEWIS

THE
History
PRESS

Published by The History Press
Charleston, SC
www.historypress.com

First published 2023

Manufactured in the United States

ISBN 9781467153706

Library of Congress Control Number: 2023932154

Notice: The information in this book is true and complete to the best of our knowledge. It is offered without guarantee on the part of the author or The History Press. The author and The History Press disclaim all liability in connection with the use of this book.

In loving memory of my stepson, Daniel Jon DeVries.

CONTENTS

ACKNOWLEDGEMENTS

This and previous projects would not have been possible without the resources found in the amazing libraries, museums and historical societies around the state. A huge thank-you to Marla Barnes, the audiovisual archivist at the Walter Ruether Library at Wayne State University, and to Carla Reczek for providing images from the Burton Historical Collection of the Detroit Public Library. Also thanks go to Susan Hagerman and the museum committee at the Bath School Museum. Thank you, too, to Annakathryn Parker Welch at the State Library of Michigan and the local and state history collection at the Grand Rapids Public Library. Without your heroic efforts, Michigan's rich history would be lost.

Special thanks to Mark Thompson, who until his 2022 retirement served as director of Presque Isle Historical Museum and who has done an outstanding job of unraveling the true story behind all the incorrect information floating around about Albert Molitor. Thank you for letting me use your material.

To John Rodrigue, acquisitions editor extraordinaire; project editor Ryan Finn; the production pros; the sales and marketing teams; and all the unsung heroes at Arcadia Publishing/The History Press who make doing these books a joy.

Also, a big shout-out to all the history buffs and nostalgia buffs who read these books. I so enjoy meeting and talking with you, and one of my biggest thrills is when someone recognizes a family member or has a connection to the book. Without readers, there would be no need for books. You're the best!

Thanks again to my granddaughter Shelby Ayers for gently guiding me through all the technological glitches that constantly plague me. Always last, but never least, thank you to the rest of my family and friends, who not only support and encourage me in these endeavors but also put with my occasional craziness while the work is in process. I love you!

INTRODUCTION

While hunting for scoundrels for this book, a question naturally arose: Are scoundrels born or made? At least one of the scoundrels herein also pondered the question and concluded that they are made. Andrew Kehoe had no doubt that a series of seemingly insurmountable obstacles led him to plan and carry out the nation's first school bombing. He not only believed that scoundrels are made, but he also left behind a handwritten sign saying so. Conversely, sticky-fingered Silas Doty chose the path he would follow while still in early childhood. By the time he was nine, he had graduated from stealing from his siblings and figured out that if he stole some, but not all, of the animals caught by local trappers, he could earn money by selling the pelts without drawing suspicion to himself. He obviously was not your typical nine-year-old.

One common trait among many of them was the belief that they were destined for greatness. Dr. John Harvey Kellogg knew that he would become a doctor and that he would live his life in the public eye. His brother, William Keith, attained as much success but chose to work out of the spotlight. That should have made for a smooth partnership, but each harbored a distrust and thinly veiled dislike of the other. A major disagreement was whether or not their corn flakes should be made available to the public at large. Had William Keith not prevailed, what would our children eat for breakfast?

That inner conviction that the world stage awaited made Benjamin Purnell establish the Israelite House of David. It was easy for James Jesse Strang to form his own ragtag Mormon band of followers. All he had to do was dig up (literally!) proof that he was the chosen prophet. Supposedly an angel told him where to dig, but he really didn't need that assistance, as he'd forged and buried the so-called proof himself. But even that prophet status wasn't quite enough—he had himself crowned king as well.

And he wasn't Michigan's only self-proclaimed monarch. The other, Albert Molitor, was believed by some to have royal blood. He didn't. After leaving his native Germany amid accusations of treason, he ended up in what he considered a ruling position in Rogers City. When he famously referred to a group of detractors as "peasants," it was obvious that he considered himself to be of a much higher social class.

Jim Bakker didn't decide that he wanted to be a preacher—he decided that he wanted to be a televangelist. More glory, yes, but even more important to Jim, more publicity and more money!

Jimmy Hoffa achieved great power, but he was unable to resist abusing that power. We still don't know what happened to him on that day he went to lunch, never to be seen again. Although theories abound, there's an excellent chance we never will.

Robert L. Vesco was a draftsman working at the Reynolds Metals Company sales office in Detroit when he realized that he could raise his income exponentially by becoming a financial industry con man. The career change worked well for him, until the inevitable happened. He was caught. This wasn't all bad, as he spent the remainder of his life living it up in choice spots around the world. In short, he could be found on any of the multiple playgrounds for the rich and famous that lacked an extradition agreement with the United States.

When we think of westward expansion, we tend to think of covered wagons, Lewis and Clark, the transcontinental railroad and Manifest Destiny. It's easy to forget that the first westward expansion meant taming the wild and woolly midwestern states, including Michigan. Although neither John Wayne nor Clint Eastwood ever depicted that era in movies, some of the same elements existed right here on Michigan soil.

Michigan had saloon brawls, brothels, mining disputes and bank robberies like any other frontier. Dan Seavey thoroughly enjoyed saloon brawling and also operated a floating brothel. Of course, not all Michigan bank robbers robbed Michigan banks. The Muskegon Bidwell brothers, along with two accomplices, managed what was previously thought to be impossible. After practicing around Europe, they stole a fortune from the Bank of England, thought to be one of the world's most secure financial institutions.

The Bidwells and Robert Vesco committed their financial crimes more than a century apart, but both operations required high levels of skill, boldness and intelligence to carry out. That makes for an interesting question. Had they put their talents into creating wealth honestly, instead of venturing down what the Bidwells called the "Primrose Way," could they have done even better?

So sit back and enjoy the ride. From garden-variety scofflaws to a few kingpins of organized crime and everything in between, you're about to meet the best of the worst in Michigan's history. Some of their shenanigans are funny in retrospect but probably were not at all amusing at the time. Others were then, and always will be, tragic.

A CHRISTMAS EVE TRAGEDY

*The mining industry might make wealth and power for a few men and women,
but the many would always be smashed and battered beneath its giant treads.*
—Katherine Susannah Prichard

Although the tragedy unfolded on December 24, 1913, the trouble had been brewing since the previous summer. Red Jacket, Michigan, one of the mining towns in the Keweenaw Peninsula, in Upper Peninsula Michigan's copper country, was home to the Calumet and Hecla Mining Company, the leading copper producer in the United States and, from 1869 to 1876, the leading producer in the world.

James MacNaughton managed the mines and employed nearly all the men in the area. Most were immigrants who had flocked to the Keweenaw to work. Those from Ireland and England's Cornwall were the only ones who spoke and understood English. Others came from Italy, Poland, Hungary and Croatia, but the majority hailed from Finland. The international miners hung out with their own countrymen and even published newspapers in their native languages.

Most of them were happy to have jobs that enabled them to take care of their families. One benefit was that the company owned houses that employees could rent. The downside was that what the company could give, it could also arbitrarily take away.

In the twenty-first century, with the Occupational Safety and Health Administration regulating the workplace, atrocities like those the miners faced seem hard to believe. Accidents causing serious injury or death were everyday occurrences. They came from careless use of explosives, fires, falls or being bonked on the head by a falling rock. Sometimes the stricken could file and win a lawsuit, but clearly the miners needed more support than was usually at their disposal.

Copper miners in Colorado already had that assistance. It came in the form of the Western Federation of Miners, a labor union. If there was one thing James MacNaughton hated, it was organized labor. He did have one legitimate reason for that hatred, as he had once been the intended target in a WFM assassination plot.

MacNaughton's goal was to make sure unionization didn't happen in the Michigan copper mines—at least not on his watch. Toward that end, he spied on his employees, often hiring Pinkerton operatives or detectives from other agencies to report back to him any miners they heard talking about organizing. In at least one instance, that ploy had an unintended consequence. After seeing firsthand how bad the working conditions really were, the would-be informant sided with the miners.

In his defense, MacNaughton genuinely cared for the men he employed and felt a keen responsibility toward their welfare. He was convinced that they fared better under his paternalistic style of management than they would under union representation. To some extent, he was right. They earned higher wages than most miners and lived independently. While some chose to rent company-owned houses, many owned their own homes. None were forced to buy their groceries and other necessities at inflated prices at company-owned stores. There were no such stores in Red Jacket. Local merchants prospered under the status quo and also opposed unionization.

Despite all the positives in this better-than-most situation, the WFA gained a foothold in Red Jacket, and slightly less than half of the miners became WFA members.

On July 23, 1913, they voted to strike. The issues were legitimate: safer working conditions, shorter hours and more pay. Management refused to recognize the strike and failed to meet with the strikers. To them, and most of the townspeople agreed, the union wasn't legal, as the majority of miners had chosen not to join. Also, less than half of the members voted to strike. It's probably safe to say that they would have ignored the strike had there been 100 percent membership and *all* of them supported the strike.

ANNIE CLEMENC   HEROINE OF THE
MICH COPPER COUNTRY STRIKE 1913

Left: "Big Annie" Clemenc worked tirelessly on behalf of the striking miners and their families. *Michigan Women's Hall of Fame.*

Below: Calumet's Italian Hall, the scene of the Christmas Eve children's party. *Detroit Public Library.*

Once the strike started, neutrality was not an option. Most of the town lined up behind the mine owners. As Congressman William MacDonald said, "You are either with the mine owners or you're against them." He was with them as well.

Scabs, including non-union member employees, worked the mines, while the strikers often were beaten. The National Guard appeared on the scene, and guardsmen also targeted "anyone carrying a lunch pail," as one journalist reported. Ana Clemenc, wife of a Croatian striker, showed her support for the strikers by marching every day carrying an oversized American flag. Called "Big Annie" because she stood at six-foot-two, she also attacked scabs on a few occasions. Her heroic actions during the 1913 strike led to her being arrested a few times. It also led to her being the first woman to be inducted into the Michigan Women's Hall of Fame.

Annie became concerned when it drew close to Christmas with still no end in sight. Everyone knew that Red Jacket would not be part of Santa's Christmas Eve itinerary and that the children would be facing a bleak holiday. Annie wanted to help, so she organized a children's holiday party to help ease their disappointment. The event would be held on Christmas Eve at the Italian Mutual Benefit Society building, known informally as the Italian Hall.

The hall was a two-story building with a saloon and an Atlantic & Pacific Tea Company grocery store on the first floor. The upper floor held a stage and theater seating on one side and an open hall for gatherings on the other. Annie had collected money for the children and bought candy, along with gifts like mittens and small toys. About six hundred children showed up for the festivities, along with than one hundred adults.

Two scraggly Christmas trees adorned the stage, where the gifts were stacked. Some of the kids went home after receiving their presents. Others hung around. It was, after all, a party, and there had been little for them to celebrate since July. A man wearing his hat pulled down over his face to hide his identity and a Citizen's Alliance button on his coat entered the building and yelled "Fire!" The Citizen's Alliance was a local group of townspeople who supported the mine owners.

A few ignored the warning at first, but when it had been repeated in every language represented in the hall, nearly everyone headed for the stairs to the front door. There was a fire escape at the back and also ladders propped up against the building, but most didn't know that and followed the stampede, panic-stricken. Some lost their footing and fell, causing others to fall and pile up on the stairs. When people outside the building realized what had happened, they broke down the door and pulled the victims, mostly children,

Animosity between strikers and mine owners inadvertently caused one of the worst tragedies in Michigan history. *Detroit Public Library.*

from the pile. Some were still alive. Bodies were carried back upstairs and laid out for identification. A total of seventy-three people died that day, sixty-two children and eleven adults.

Much of the information reported immediately following was incorrect. Considering the language difficulties, there was much room for misunderstanding. Because many of the witnesses were children, their versions also tended to be unreliable. As time passed, they confused what they had actually seen with what they had heard other people say—or, even worse, what they may have seen in their nightmares.

Rumors quickly spread. One was that the door opened inward, making it impossible to open with people piled up on the stairs. That has been thoroughly debunked. It was said too that the man who yelled fire had sprayed noxious gas in the hall or that he had sprayed something slippery on the stairs. Neither is true. It was also suspected by some that the enemies of the strikers had deliberately caused the catastrophe. Not true. No matter how much they may have hated their fathers, the worst of the worst would not have killed the innocent children. The entire town of Red Jacket and the surrounding communities rallied around the survivors, helped them bury their dead and joined them in mourning their losses.

Each year, the Calumet Rotary Club memorializes the tragedy by installing seventy-three luminaries, one for each victim, along a path in the park where the Italian Hall once stood.

The Upper Peninsula town of Calumet, originally named Red Jacket, mourns the deaths of the seventy-three victims of the Christmas Eve massacre. *Detroit Public Library.*

Folk singer Woody Guthrie wrote a hit song called "1913 Massacre":

Take a trip with me in nineteen thirteen
to Calumet, Michigan, in the copper country.
I'll take you to a place called Italian Hall
and the miners are having their big Christmas ball.
I'll take you in a door and up a high stairs
Singing and dancing is heard e'rywhere
I'll let you shake hands with the people you see
and watch the kids dance 'round the big Christmas tree.
There's talking and laughing and songs in the air
And the spirit of Christmas is there e'rywhere
Before you know it you're friends with us all
And you're dancing around and around in the hall
You ask about work and you ask about pay
They'll tell you they make less than a dollar a day
Working their copper claims, risking their lives
So it's fun to spend Christmas with children and wives
A little girl sits down by the Christmas tree lights
To play the piano so you gotta keep quiet
To hear all this fun; you would not realize
That the copper boss thug men are milling outside
The copper boss thugs stick their heads in the door
One of them yelled and he screamed, "There's a fire"
A lady she hollered, "There's no such a thing
Keep on with your party, there's no such a thing."
A few people rushed and there's only a few
"It's just the thugs and the scabs fooling you"
A man grabbed his daughter and he carried her down
But the thugs held the door and he could not get out
And then others followed, about a hundred or more
But most everybody remained on the floor
The gun thugs they laughed at their murderous joke
And the children were smothered on the stairs by the door
Such a terrible sight I never did see
We carried our children back up to their tree
The scabs outside still laughed at their spree
And the children that died there was seventy-three
The piano played a slow funeral tune

And the town was lit up by a cold Christmas moon
The parents they cried, and the men, they moaned,
"See what your greed for money has done?"

It raised all the righteous indignation he intended, but many parts were embellished or downright incorrect:

- The party was not a ball—it was a party planned for the benefit of the striking miners' children to provide them with treats and modest gifts that were all most of them would receive that year.
- Like the gifts Annie Clemenc managed to acquire, the two trees on the stage were modest, more of the scruffy "Charlie Brown" variety.
- Miners averaged three dollars a day, not one, which was slightly higher than most of the other mine owners paid. Pay rates were based on the work—those with the most dangerous jobs received slightly more than the general laborers.
- No one held the door closed to intentionally trap attendees.
- No one laughed at the deaths occurring inside the building. Far from it, the most rabid of the anti-union activists were horrified by what happened and genuinely grieved the horrific deaths.

The Calumet and Hecla Mine employed most of the men in town. *Detroit Public Library.*

An arch from the Italian Hall serves as a reminder of the tragedy that occurred inside its doors. *Library of Congress.*

Guthrie wrote the song to support his own political leanings and to cause outrage in the public at large at the expense of the innocent victims. He was successful enough that Bob Dylan performed the song at Carnegie Hall in 1961, complete with all the inaccuracies.

Steve Lehto is the author of the exhaustively researched *Death's Door*, the definitive book about the tragedy and the events leading up to it, and he also has roots in the area. He concluded that an unknown Citizen's Alliance member yelled "Fire!" not to set in motion the horror that followed but simply to add a bit of stress to the strikers' party.

That begs the question of why was that individual never found and charged? Whether intentional or not, he had caused unthinkable pain. Rewards were offered. There have even been a few deathbed confessions. But none could be verified, mainly because those confessions were never the confessions of the perpetrator, but of someone to whom the guilty party had allegedly unburdened himself.

AMERICA'S FIRST

SCHOOL BOMBING AND DEADLIEST SCHOOL MASSACRE

Criminals are made, not born.
—Andrew Kehoe

Andrew Philip Kehoe was born on February 1, 1872, on a farm in Tecumseh, Michigan. Even in childhood, he distinguished himself as a tinkerer, always working on, and often improving, the family's farming machinery.

It naturally followed that he would continue his education by studying electrical engineering at Michigan State College, now Michigan State University. Following college, he went to St. Louis, Missouri, where he found work as an electrician. While there, Kehoe suffered a fall in which he sustained a head injury serious enough to leave him comatose for two weeks. After recuperating, he returned to the family farm in Tecumseh. Unfortunately, during his absence, things had changed significantly back home, and the changes were not to his liking.

Andrew Kehoe had shown signs of a deeply troubled and dangerously flawed individual, but the signs had gone unrecognized.

He was still an obsessive tinkerer, and that made him a loner, essentially living in his head and oblivious to the larger world around him. His mother had died, and his father, Philip, married Frances Wilder, a woman Andrew hated. The feeling was mutual.

Frannie died an agonizing death as the result of a kitchen fire. When the story of the Bath school massacre became known, the folks back in Tecumseh wondered if Andrew was responsible for Frannie's death as well. There had been rumors at the time that the stove had been tampered with. Andrew's innate mechanical ability, coupled with his formal education, would have given him the know-how.

When Frannie struck a match to light the oil stove to make lunch, it exploded. With her clothes aflame, she ran frantically around the kitchen, screaming and trying to put the fire out. Andrew responded to her anguished cries by throwing a pitcher of water on her. Because it was an oil fire, that only made it worse.

Eventually, the flames were extinguished. The family had no telephone, so Andrew was sent to a neighboring farm to call the doctor. The neighbor later reported that Andrew showed no sense of urgency and chatted nonchalantly until the neighbor finally asked the reason for his unexpected visit. Farm dwellers are too busy to engage in idle chitchat in the middle of the day.

"Frannie burned herself and thinks she needs to see the doctor," he eventually said, trivializing the accident and making no attempt to hide his smirk. As a devout Irish Catholic, Frannie had also asked that a priest be summoned. That added request makes it sound as if Andrew should have understood the gravity of the situation.

The doctor came, but Frannie was burned too badly for effective treatment and died a few hours later. The priest also came and was able to deliver last rites before she succumbed to her injuries.

Andrew would have known how to tamper with the stove and cause the explosion directly. At the very least, the way he handled the situation made it worse. He should have known that water would accelerate the flames, and his indifference to her suffering showed a complete lack of compassion.

While at college, Andrew met Ellen (Nellie) Price, and the two married a few years later. They moved to a farm they bought from Nellie's aunt for a total of $12,000. After paying half down, they mortgaged the $6,000 balance.

There was no doubt that Andrew Kehoe was intelligent, but he was incapable of making that intelligence work for him. He had farmed with his father in Tecumseh and then he and Nellie had their own farm in Bath, but he never got the hang of doing it successfully. Acquaintances said that he was more interested in tinkering with machinery than actually doing the hard work involved. When seen driving his tractor, he was dressed more like a banker than a farmer, and he went so far as to change his shirt at least once during the day. Folks who had seen them also claimed that Andrew Kehoe's barns were as clean some people's kitchens.

Andrew was known for being tightfisted with money. A prime example was the Kehoes' church attendance. Both were Catholic, and they regularly attended Mass at the local Catholic church. That came to an abrupt halt when he was asked to support the church financially. He never went back and insisted Nellie boycott the church as well.

Another thing he railed against was taxation of any kind. School taxes especially enraged him. The district had recently closed all the individual one-room schools in favor of a new consolidated school, a move he felt was financially foolhardy. When a new tax was levied to pay for the structure, he rallied against it. He and Nellie had no children, so why should they be forced to pay for a school that, in his opinion, never should have been built?

In the end, all his attempts to have the tax repealed failed. He then claimed that the tax would ruin him financially, so he asked for, and was given, a part-time job as the school custodian. When he was seen doing electrical work at the school, people shrugged it off, saying that he was just too miserly to spend money on an electrician even though it would have been the school's money not his own.

The whole school situation motivated him to run for a spot on the Bath Consolidated School Board. Serving on the board, and eventually being elected to the position of treasurer, raised his standing in the community. His meticulously kept books gave him the grudging respect of other board members. But he was still seen as an obstructionist and proved many times to be as miserly with the school's money as he was with his own. He perceived Emory Hyuck, the school superintendent, as an enemy and tried to have him barred from attending meetings. That failed, so did the next best thing and fought him at every turn.

He felt that Hyuck was financially irresponsible, always lobbying for more and better equipment in the boys' shop and girls' home economics rooms. He even asked that funds be allocated for new playground equipment. Kehoe considered those expenditures frivolous and always spoke up against them. If the rest of the board appeared ready to support the expense, he made a motion to adjourn the meeting before a vote could be taken.

He was known as a good neighbor and willing to help when needed, especially if that help involved the use of explosives, the preferred method for removing tree stumps. Even so, there was something off about him. People respected his intelligence and attention to detail but never really warmed up to him. For one thing, he was known to be cruel to animals. In a fit of temper, he beat one of his horses to death, and he also admitted to killing a neighbor's dog just because he considered the mutt a nuisance.

Another suspicious characteristic was his fascination with explosives. In 1924, he celebrated the Fourth of July with fireworks the likes of which had never before been seen in the small city of Bath. Some people were frightened, but to others it was just Andrew being Andrew. When neighbors complained to Nellie, she was quick to defend her husband. "The little boy is just having some fun," she said to calm their fears. It's unknown if he heard that remark or how he felt about his own wife publicly referring to him as a little boy.

By 1927, Andrew Kehoe's problems were mounting at an alarming rate. He had fallen behind in his mortgage payments and his homeowner's insurance premiums. Nellie's incurable tuberculosis required frequent hospitalizations. The escalating medical bills piled up.

He became convinced that his mortgage was about to be foreclosed. Nellie's aunt held the mortgage, and that would never have happened, especially with Nellie's chronic health issues. But Andrew refused to believe those who told him that he didn't have to worry about it. Also, what little power he had in the community was quickly eroding. He was serving his last term on the school board. He had been appointed the interim town clerk but lost the general election to keep the position.

Kehoe's bitterness boiled over, and any last shred of reason evaporated. In his tortured mind, there was only one solution: make those who had ruined his life pay. Sadly, most of those who paid were the thirty-eight innocent children who had nothing at all to do with his mounting troubles.

On May 17, 1927, the school's trusted custodian went to the school, where he wired three hundred pounds of dynamite, the agricultural explosive phytol and blasting caps in the basement. The next morning sent shock waves through the community when two separate explosions occurred at the school. People hurried to the site to see what had happened and to do whatever they could to help those who were injured. Kehoe himself drove to the scene. One woman he passed on the way later said that he had waved at her and tipped his hat. A monster in disguise, yes, but polite to the end.

At the schoolyard, he spotted his hated adversary, Emory Hyuck, and motioned him over to the car. The unsuspecting superintendent probably assumed that Kehoe was there to help and sat beside Kehoe on the front seat. Then Kehoe picked up his gun and fired into a pile of dynamite in the back of the car. The resulting blast blew up the car, instantly killing Huyck, Kehoe, a young boy who had already survived one of the earlier explosions and four more. He had killed his wife, Nellie, the day before—when police went to the farm, they found Nellie dead. Also dead were the Kehoes' horses. Propped up against the fence, they found a hand-lettered sign that read "Criminals are made not born."

After the tragedy, some wondered if he had sustained significant brain damage in his fall in St. Louis that led to his later behavior. Highly unlikely, as Kehoe exhibited enough of the classic symptoms of a psychopath to pose as the psychiatric disorder's poster child: an inability to feel guilt or remorse, a limited range of emotions, a lack of empathy, behaving irresponsibly, acting impulsively and the inability to control his often irrational behavior.

When people heard about the disaster and that Kehoe was the man responsible, someone remembered that he had earlier been insistent that a package be delivered to the post office. Fearing the worst, police stormed the building and removed the suspicious package. Outside, they carefully opened it, only to find it contained the Bath Consolidated School District accounting ledger. Treasurer Andrew Kehoe had placed his bookkeeping in the mail, meticulously balanced as always.

The final death toll was forty-five: three men, three women (including Nellie), thirty-eight children and Andrew Kehoe himself. The Ku Klux Klan responded to the mass murders by distributing 5 million propaganda leaflets in Michigan. The leaflets blamed the tragedy entirely on Kehoe's Catholic upbringing.

The Bath Consolidated School after Andrew Kehoe executed the country's first school bombing. *Michigan History Center.*

In the aftermath of such suffering, it sounds insensitive to say that it could have been worse—Andrew Kehoe had intended for it to be. Part of the investigation that followed included searching what was left of the school. Authorities found that one whole section of the school had been wired to explode, but it had miraculously failed to detonate.

The nation's next three deadliest school massacres were all shootings. On April 16, 2007, Seung-Hui Cho, a twenty-three-year-old student at Virginia Polytechnic Institute and State University in Blacksburg, Virginia, opened fire at the school and killed twenty-five students and five faculty members. The Sandy Hook Elementary School killings in Newtown, Connecticut, took place on December 14, 2012, when a twenty-year-old former student named Adam Lanza shot and killed twenty first-grade students, four teachers, the principal, the school psychologist and himself. The most recent happened on May 24, 2022, when eighteen-year-old Salvador Ramos killed nineteen students and two teachers at the Robb Elementary School in Uvalde, Texas. Earlier that day, he had killed his grandmother. Ramos was killed by a tactical team of U.S. Border Patrol agents.

A BAD DAY IN GOOD HART

When that crime happened, the innocence of Northern Michigan was shattered, in a way, and it took years for that to dissipate.
—*Mardi Link, true crime author of* When Evil Came to Good Hart

The Robison family of six—father Richard, forty-two; mother Shirley, forty; Ritchie, nineteen; Gary, sixteen; Randall, twelve; and Susan, seven—lived the American dream in the upscale Metropolitan Detroit suburb of Lathrop Village. Richard owned an advertising business in Southfield, where he also published an art magazine, *impresario*. Shirley was a homemaker.

Their affluence made it possible to also own a vacation home, a luxurious log cabin on Lake Michigan at Good Hart, near the Straits of Mackinac. The cabin was built of fieldstone and varnished logs. Good Hart, in Emmett County, looked like the perfect place for a hardworking businessman to chill out with his family. With fewer than six hundred residents, it exuded tranquility and was located in the scenic Michigan Highway 119 Tunnel of Trees.

The unincorporated township had once been home to a tribe of Ojibwes, headed by Joseph Black Hawk and his brother Good Heart, hence the name. All the Ojibwes had left the area by 1905, and it became a seasonal tourist destination, as well as a perfect spot for vacation homes for families like the Robisons.

They named the cabin Summerset, and except for short trips to Florida and Kentucky, that's where they had planned to spend the remainder of the

The beautiful Tunnel of Trees near Harbor Springs in northern Michigan, near where members of the Robison family were murdered. *Wikimedia Commons.*

summer of 1968. It was not to be. The entire family was brutally murdered on June 25, all shot to death. Richard and seven-year-old Susan were also bludgeoned with a hammer found at the scene.

The bodies were not found until twenty-seven days later when someone complained of a horrible stench in the woods behind the family's home. The Robison's caretaker, Monty Bliss, unlocked the door, and the first thing he saw was Shirley's body. He looked no further and immediately called the Emmett County Sheriff's Office.

The investigation went on for fifteen months, with no arrest and no suspect publicly named. Police decided early on that this had to be the work of someone with whom Richard had business dealings. The family was well liked and respected and had no known enemies. Immediate and extended family members had no conflicts with one another. Monty Bliss was briefly considered a suspect but quickly eliminated.

A few things were stolen, but the robbery-gone-bad scenario was never one the police seriously considered. Shirley's diamond ring, valued at $9,000, was missing, along with a string of pearls and Richard's Omega wristwatch. Also missing from the scene was the cash he had just withdrawn from the bank. A thief would not have overlooked the cameras, electronics and other valuables the police found in the house.

The Good Hart General Store, the only retail business in the area. *Norma Lewis collection.*

The investigation proved that Robison was not the squeaky-clean businessman he was first thought to be. He overcharged some of his clients, including the largest, the Delta Faucet Company; however, that was quickly dismissed as a motive for murder. Corporations settle their differences by filing lawsuits and taking their business elsewhere, not by resorting to violence. His magazine was not what it appeared to be either, as he included advertisements for companies (including Delta Faucet) that he created himself, without the companies' knowledge. The ads were his means of giving the publication a credibility it lacked.

The Robisons' marriage was not what it seemed either, as Robison had engaged in multiple affairs. When his secretary became pregnant, he was rumored to be the father. She miscarried, so a paternity test was never done. That led to more rumors, as her boyfriend was known to have Detroit mafia connections. The boyfriend-seeking-revenge scenario was also dismissed, as he could well have been the father, and all the evidence pointed elsewhere. Also, mob murders are done with a level of expertise that was clearly lacking in Good Hart.

One business associate, Richard's employee Joseph Raymond Scolaro III, soon emerged as the prime suspect. According to some sources, he was actually a partner, not an employee, but either way he had the opportunity, motive and means. While all the evidence was circumstantial, it was compelling, and there was a staggering amount of it.

Scolaro was embezzling money from Richard Robison's company. No one had seen him or could account for his whereabouts on the day of the murder. He was not in his office, and according to his wife, he didn't return home until around 10:00 p.m. that day. His alibis couldn't be verified. He had bought the two murder weapons—a .25-caliber Jet-Fire automatic Beretta pistol and a .22-caliber AR-7 Arma-Lite semi-automatic rifle. Shell casings found at the crime scene were an exact match to those he had fired at his father-in-law's firing range the year before. His boots perfectly matched prints left at the scene. His boots were brand new and still in the box, but he had a habit of buying two of everything, so it was suspected that he had discarded his bloodstained boots. He failed two lie detector tests. Seventeen phone calls occurred between Richard and Joseph shortly before the murders, leaving police to wonder if Richard had discovered the missing money.

In at least one of those calls, Richard wanted to know if a missing $200,000 check had been deposited. Also, Robison's bank had notified him that $60,000 was missing. The receptionist who answered the phone when Robison called about the missing money later reported that he was furious.

Someone coined the word *bezzle* to describe that golden window of time when the thief has the money and the owner is not yet aware that it is gone. Were the missing funds, totaling $260,000, part of the money Scolaro had stolen? And if it was, did it confirm to Scolaro that his "bezzle" window was fast slamming shut and that he had to act quickly before Richard called the police? Yes, the murder was premeditated, but was it also of such sudden urgency that it caused Scolaro to do such a poor job of covering his tracks?

A forensic audit performed on Robison's business after the murders showed that money had not started disappearing from the company coffers until after Scolaro began working there. Most embezzlers consider the stolen funds an unauthorized "loan" that they will pay back before the theft is discovered. Despite those good intentions, it seldom happens. It's too difficult to resist the urge to continue "borrowing" until the amount owed escalates to the point of no return.

On March 8, 1973, Joseph Scaloro took what must have seemed to him the only way out. Knowing that his arrest was imminent, he committed suicide before he could be charged with the heinous crimes. He left a typewritten suicide letter with a handwritten note to his mother scribbled on the bottom:

"I had nothing to do with the Robisons. I'm a liar and a cheat, but not a murderer. I'm sick and I'm tired. God and everyone else forgive me."

Scolaro's suicide saved the State of Michigan the time and the money a trial would have cost, but it also meant that those who loved the Robisons would never have the satisfaction of seeing him convicted and made to pay for what he had done. The case is permanently labeled unsolved and inactive. That said, authorities have no doubts at all about who murdered the family, but with the perpetrator dead, there is nothing more they can do.

A DARK TIME
IN MICHIGAN HISTORY

Hate, it has caused a lot of problems in this world, but it has not solved one yet.
—Maya Angelou

It may be hard to believe that there could ever have been an organized hate group even more vicious than the Ku Klux Klan, but there was. The 1930s saw the appearance of a secret society called the Black Legion. It hated the same people the Klan hated but hated them even more. It has also been compared to the Molly Maguires, a secret society originating in Ireland and in the English Liverpool area organized to brutally respond to the mistreatment and discrimination of Irish miners.

The Irish potato famine brought more than 1 million Irish immigrants to the United States. The Molly Maguires popped up in the anthracite coal mining region of Pennsylvania. Irish immigrants faced double discrimination, as they were Catholic as well as Irish. This happened during the last half of the nineteenth century, when "Help Wanted" signs usually included the wording "Irish need not apply." The Molly Maguires themselves were offshoots of earlier hate groups including the Whiteboys and the Ribbonmen, so the KKK and the Black Legion were not groundbreaking. There have always been such organizations, and unfortunately, there probably always will be.

The Black Legion operated in the Midwest, primarily in Michigan and Ohio and to a lesser degree in Illinois and Indiana. The Legion was organized like a quasi-military operation and divided into 5 brigades, 16 regiments, 64 battalions and 256 companies. Members were required to recruit new members by inviting them to what they called a political meeting. Upon arrival, the recruits were sworn in at gunpoint and made to repeat an oath of allegiance:

> *In the power of God and the devil and the power of light and darkness, goodness and evil, under the black arch of heaven's avenging symbol, I pledge and consecrate my heart, my brain, my body and limbs; and I swear by all the perseverance of heaven and hell, to devote my life to the obedience of my superiors that I will exert every possible means in my power for the extermination of the antichrist, Communist, the Roman hierarchy, and their abettors.*

Who would take such an oath? The short answer: any man with the barrel of a gun pressed against his head.

As if to drive home the fact that this was a permanent commitment, the swearing-in ceremony was at the same time a punishment venue where those who had failed to live up to their oath were beaten. If there were no members currently in need of flogging, the beatings were staged. "Let's make sure these new recruits don't get any ideas" seemed to be the rationale.

Bert Effingham, a maniacal communist-fearing electrician in Lima, Ohio, founded the group. Among his Death Squad enforcers in Michigan were Dayton Dean, a major, and Lowell Rushing and Harvey Davis, colonels and triggermen, all of whom were living in the Detroit area. Colonel Davis has been described as "a tall, lanky, rat-faced creature." Most of the rank-and-file membership consisted of uneducated southerners, sometimes referred to as rednecks, who had come north for factory jobs in the automotive industry. The Federal Bureau of Investigation called them hillbillies. They were living in a big city for the first time ever and felt intimidated. Also intimidating was the idea of working with a diverse population, another first for those involved.

The group was also known by other names, including the Black Guard, Black Knights and the Black Night Riders. Unlike the Klan's white robes, the Legion's robes were black, and their hats were adorned with the pirate's skull and crossbones icon. Those who may have had second thoughts about the organization had no recourse. If they thought they could put it all behind them by not attending meetings, they soon leaned otherwise. Thug enforcers who didn't beat them at swearing-in ceremonies drove them to marshes and other secluded areas, where they administered beatings that sent the offenders home with long, bleeding gashes on their backs.

Complaining to law enforcement agencies was not an option, as all had been infiltrated by Legion members. The person to whom you complained just might be the one you were complaining about, and the risk of retaliation in the form of death or a brutal beating was just too great.

Known infiltrators included dozens of police officers; the police chief of Royal Oak; Duncan McRae, Wayne County prosecutor, whose corruption was common knowledge; at least one state legislator; one county prosecutor; and close to one hundred other elected or appointed public officials. Even the Detroit chief of police was suspected of being a member. High-profile members were especially desirable. Mickey Cochrane, the Detroit Tigers baseball team's new player and manager, was highly sought after. While he managed to avoid being shanghaied into joining, the stress led to his having a nervous breakdown. At its peak, membership was estimated at about 500,000, but that figure was probably inflated, with the actual number being closer to 300,000.

They claimed to be American patriots, and like the Klan, they hated Black people, Catholics, Jews, unions, fraternal groups and immigrants. Even their own members weren't entirely safe. One man refused to divorce his Catholic wife. Higher-ups in the Legion were master manipulators and convinced flunkies that he was abusing his children. Such a man should be killed, they reasoned; then they sat back and waited for the deed to be done.

The Michigan contingent of the Legion is believed to have been responsible for at least fifty murders, but the actual body count could be much higher, as some may have been mistakenly recorded as suicides. It would be an easy mistake to make, as many of the killings were intentionally staged to look like suicides. To their shame, investigators often failed to investigate deaths in the Black communities. The prevailing attitude seemed to be "These people seem bent on killing each other. Let's not get involved."

Harvey Davis was a U.S. Navy veteran and divorced from his wife, who claimed physical abuse and cruelty. He next lived with a woman who ended the relationship when she found out that he had sexually abused her fourteen-year-old daughter. He admitted that the Legion caused the shooting of a Black man who became a victim simply because he was in the wrong place at the wrong time. He inadvertently crossed paths with a group of assassins who felt frustrated when they were unable to find the man they had gone out to kill that night. Already primed to kill, they took out their disappointment on the first man they saw. Ecorse mayor William W. (Bill) Voisine had been the original target. Voisine, both an immigrant and a Catholic, already had two strikes against him. He sealed his fate with the practice of adding

Black people, immigrants and other undesirables to the city payroll. He was popular with his constituents and served seven terms before his death on December 27, 1959. It's thought that he knew someone wanted him dead and was able to stay out of harm's way.

Roy Pidcock was taken on a one-way ride because he refused to leave his Catholic common-law wife, Nellie. He couldn't divorce her because they were not legally married and wouldn't have anyway. They had two children together, and he was a loving father figure to her other four children. One can only imagine his distress when he was forced at gunpoint to join an organization known for hating the religious denomination to which his beloved Nellie belonged.

But it was the notorious Charles Poole murder that demonstrated just how evil this group really was. It finally not only penetrated the layers of secrecy but also laid it bare for the public to view. Humphrey Bogart starred in a movie that was loosely based on the Poole case, drawing even more attention to the repugnant Legion.

In the movie, Bogart's character is an automotive industry worker who expects to be promoted to shop foreman. When the promotion is instead given to a Polish immigrant, the man joins the Black Legion to exact revenge, feeling that he has been wronged.

The real Poole was marked for death by the revenge-seeking Lowell Rushing, who was the brother-in-law of Charles's wife, Becky. Rushing had met Becky years earlier and had fallen in love with her long before she ever met and married Charles Poole. Meanwhile, her sister, Marcia, had married Lowell Rushing's brother, Owen.

Marcia Rushing was known for drinking too much, stretching the truth and being a troublemaker just for the fun of it. She told the friends and family members who hung out at her house that Poole treated Becky cruelly. She said he had beaten Becky so badly that she was in the hospital as the result of a miscarriage.

When later questioned about what she had said, Marcia said that it was all true. She sensed that she was in way over her head and was afraid of the likely consequences if she admitted the truth. Harvey Davis was ordered to take care of the matter. A plan was hatched, taking advantage of the fact that Poole was out of work at the time but was known as a good baseball player. He would be told that he was being taken to a meeting about a factory team that was being organized. All the large factories had company teams, and Charles Poole was led to believe that as soon as he was accepted for the team, he would automatically be hired to work in the factory.

However, there was no factory. No meeting. No ball team. No job. It was all a ruse to lure Poole into the car with the assassins. When the thugs showed up, Davis pointed out Poole, and the two got in the killers' car for another of the Black Legion's signature one-way rides.

Sadly, the more Davis talked with Poole, the more he realized that the original accusations didn't add up. Becky Poole was indeed hospitalized, but not for domestic violence. She had just given birth to the couple's second daughter. Davis saw that he was not a wife beater at all, but instead a loving husband and proud father. Any dissension in the marriage stemmed from the normal tensions a couple faces when the only breadwinner is temporarily unemployed. But as bad as Davis might have felt, he knew that there was no turning back. Orders were orders, and if he stopped the execution, Poole would still be killed. And so would Harvey Davis. Dayton Dean held a gun while Harvey Davis delivered a lecture on spousal abuse. Davis was annoyed when Dean fired the fatal shots before he had finished lecturing.

Although the Legion started as a secret society, rumors had spread and reached the FBI and J. Edgar Hoover, who at first ignored the reports, mainly due to lack of substantiating evidence of the threat. Furthermore, there was a lack of evidence that the Black Legion even existed. The reason he most often cited for not investigating was lack of jurisdiction.

The Black Legion finally imploded in 1936, and it was the murder of Charles Poole that brought it crashing down. Witnesses at the café where Poole was last seen alive fingered Harvey Davis as the man who left with Poole. Davis was arrested, and that's when the secrecy ended. He felt genuine remorse over the murder and said that it was the result of a horrible mistake; he also agreed to help bring the Legion down.

The floodgates opened as he ratted out more and more of the members. Like Davis, others became informants to save their own necks. Prison was definitely in their immediate future, but that was far more appealing than an agonizing death orchestrated by the ruthless Black Legion.

When the first Legion member was arrested, the group's long-held policy of secrecy flew out the window. More arrests quickly followed. Dayton Dean went on to describe the murder of Silas Coleman, the Black man he had chased down and shot multiple times in the back. He said that he had no animosity toward the victim, as he had never even met him. The only reason he did it was because he "wanted to see how it would feel to kill a black man."

As layer after layer of the organization's secrets were peeled away, the horrified public wanted to know how such atrocities could have happened over so long a period without being thoroughly investigated. In the end, Davis's testimony led to charges being filed against more than fifty members. In a series of trials held during 1936 and 1937, forty-six were convicted in four separate trials of felonies up to and including murder.

Dayton Dean died of a heart attack in 1960 while incarcerated. He had served twenty-four years of a life sentence.

THE STICKIEST FINGERS
IN ALL OF MICHIGAN

Stealing, you'll go far in life.
Actually there's something funny about getting away with it.
—Mike Judge

Had there been a Nobel Prize for thievery, Silas Doty would have won hands down, or at the very least been a worthy contender. His fingers became sticky during early childhood and grew more so with the passage of time. Silas, known as Sile, was born in St. Albans, Vermont, on May 30, 1800, and was the fourth great-grandson of Edward Doty, a passenger on the *Mayflower*. Sile single-handedly took away any prestige Edward might have bestowed on the Doty family name.

Sile started in childhood by stealing toys from his brothers and sisters. But he wasn't all bad, as he sometimes let them borrow the toys back to play with them. Other times he let them play with toys but charged them rent. At age nine, he was successfully working trap lines in Maine, where the family lived at the time. He didn't work them in the traditional way the real trappers did. Knowledge is power, and he knew where they were located and when they were checked. That enabled him get there first and remove some but not all of the animals. He sold the pelts, and because he always left some dead animals behind, he was able to do this for about three years without ever arousing suspicion. Sile was precociously clever for a nine-year-old.

While still in his teens, he persuaded the local blacksmith to allow him access to his forge. There he crafted a wide array of keys of various shapes and sizes, along with a few other tools he thought would be useful in his chosen profession. He did a good job and used some of them for the rest of his life.

By the time he moved to Adrian, Michigan, in 1834, he was an accomplished thief, and he continued to improve his game. He took over his competition and created a wide-reaching organization of burglars, highwaymen and, some say, when he deemed it necessary, killers.

Although he went down in history as a gang leader, having taken over multiple ragtag bands of outlaws, it was his solo adventures that best demonstrate his creativity in turning basic chicanery into an art form—and enjoying every minute of it.

Sile left home at twenty years old. He needed to get away from his father. There had been a recent spike in local criminal activity, and his parents had a pretty good idea who might be behind the crime wave. His original plan had been to go to Buffalo, New York, and find work as a sailor. Much to his surprise and delight, he found Buffalo to be ripe for plundering. And who better to plunder? Any sailing career would have to be put on the back burner.

He started stealing horses, and that would remain his favorite enterprise. That didn't stop him from branching out into stealing money, sometimes along with the cash register the money was parked in, and anything else that found itself on the master thief's radar. Eventually, he went back to his original plan and found work sailing on the St. Lawrence Seaway. That soon became frustrating in the extreme. He was never in one place long enough to take complete advantage of all the bounty there for the taking—so much to pilfer, so little time.

Some thieves have been said to steal anything not nailed down. With self-crafted tools, creative imagination and love of a challenge, it seemed there was nothing Sile couldn't liberate once he set his mind to it. He stole anything and everything, if only because it was there for the pinching, and he was never able to walk away from a good puzzle.

He came close to getting caught on one of his early horse stealing forays. The sheriff and a posse were fast closing in on him, so he stopped at a farmhouse and told the farmer that he was a sheriff trying to track down a horse thief; he asked if he and his horse could stop there and rest. The helpful farmer put the horse in his stable and then took Sile in to enjoy a lovely meal prepared by the farmer's wife. As they leisurely enjoyed their food, the lawmen galloped by. Sile left soon after, taking with him a clock he had admired while dining.

Always seeking new areas to practice his craft, and maybe because he was again close to getting arrested, he and a temporary partner, whose last name was Wicks, sailed from Canada to England in late 1824 or early 1825. They went on a bold stealing spree that lasted about two years. They started in Liverpool and then ventured into Scotland before making their way to London. They found the Brits to be even more horse proud than the Americans and so were able to purloin some of the best horseflesh in the world.

Sile married and fathered several children. He even felt pangs of guilt and decided to go straight for a short time following the marriage, but he soon overcame that guilt and plunged right back into the profession he had long practiced and long loved. The family left Michigan and moved to a farm in Steubenville, Indiana, in 1839. He was arrested in Indiana, but the local law enforcement professionals had a hard time keeping him under wraps. It must have been hard to be sticky and slippery at the same time, but Sile proved himself equal to the task. Once, when he was unable to escape on his own, a friend visited and gifted him with a hacksaw. Bye bye, Silas Doty!

He was arrested a few more times over his career, but that only forced him to hone the newest skillset on his résumé: breaking out of jail. He was, by all accounts, a likeable chap, so his captors had a habit of not guarding him as closely as they should have. Also, they often failed to search him for hidden weapons, lock picking devices and other tools of his trade. But even he couldn't always escape and actually served a few sentences.

After being arrested in Hillsdale County on a laundry list of "charges too numerous to name," he made bail and then hightailed it to Chicago, where he began his personal best bout of crime. From there, he worked St. Louis before returning to Indiana.

Another of his crimes was passing counterfeit currency. No, he didn't steal it, but he probably could have. He bought the bills from a New York City counterfeiter named Ed Cooper. The artist sold them for thirty dollars per hundred. Maybe Sile simply admired Cooper's entrepreneurial spirit and wanted to support the effort.

Aside from thievery and spreading bogus bills, he was known to have committed a murder or three. Lorenzo G. Noyes was one of these victims. Everyone knows that farming is hard work, and Sile Doty had no experience or interest in farming or in any other form of hard work. Like most criminals, he also believed that other people were best suited for manual labor and hired Noyes to work the farm. It didn't take Noyes long to realize what his employer was really working at. That's when he made two fatal mistakes.

President James Polk gave Sile Doty a much-needed break when he declared war on Mexico. *Wikimedia Commons*.

The first was telling Sile that he was going to report him to the authorities. The hapless Mr. Noyes was apparently not overburdened with brains.

His second mistake was turning his back on Sile, who quickly grabbed a hickory branch and hit Noyes with it. When Noyes died as a result of the blow, Sile dumped the body in the swamp. It wasn't long before the body inconveniently surfaced, and Sile was charged with the murder. That was a complication he didn't need. After being jailed once again in Indiana, he once again escaped. That's when he got a completely unexpected lucky break: the United States went to war with Mexico. The government declared that the crimes committed before the war of any man who served honorably would be forgiven—yes, a get-out-of-jail-free card.

Since he was already an international thief, it stands to reason that he would want to extend his reach to Mexico when the opportunity presented itself. That opportunity came in the form of the Mexican-American War, waged from April 1846, when President James K. Polk requested Congress to declare war on Mexico to win independence for the Republic of Texas. It ended with a peace treaty on May 26, 1848. The treaty allowed the United States to buy Texas from Mexico for slightly over $18 million. Future Civil War generals fighting in the Mexican-American War included Robert E. Lee, Thomas Jonathan "Stonewall" Jackson and Ulysses S. Grant.

Sile Doty traveled to Vera Cruz, where he found General Zachary Taylor's camp and also relieved wealthy citizens of their money, jewels and other valuables. Then he found an exceptionally fine horse that he rode to Monterey and General Winfield Scott's company. He ingratiated himself with Scott by giving the horse to the general, who probably never suspected that it was stolen. Scott expressed his gratitude by giving Sile the cushy job of taking care of the beast, along with acting as a sometime messenger.

The march from Monterey to Mexico City found Sile at the top of his game. After dutifully marching all day, he disguised himself as a Mexican every night to loot and steal whatever he could get his hands on. In true Silas Doty ingenuity, he went on to sell the booty to his fellow American soldiers.

Because people liked him, many chose to make light of his profession—with some even going so far as to call him a Robin Hood who stole from the rich to give to the poor. To his credit, sometimes that is exactly what he did. If, while traveling through an area, he came upon people in need of food or other necessities, he stole what they needed and brought it back to them before continuing his travels. This naturally bought fierce loyalty and ensured that they would never rat him out to the law. He probably also

Sile Doty's Cave now has walking trails and was suspected of being a hiding place for his pilfered booty. *Library of Congress.*

charitably dispersed some of his ill-gotten goods, as he stole just because he enjoyed stealing, not because he was in need of the items.

On one known occasion, he happened upon a small ship, unattended and loaded with cargo. Score! He piloted the craft down the waterway, stopping to sell the goods wherever he could, and then sank the ship. It is believed that he hid his ill-gotten booty in a cave, but although many have searched, any buried treasure is yet to be found. He probably only used the cave to temporarily stash a multitude of stolen horses. Sile Doty's Cave now has a walking trail and is a fun place to visit.

Horses are what he stole most, often because he needed quick transportation out of town due to the impending arrival of a sheriff, a posse or both. When he was safely away from the arm of the law, he would sell the stolen horse for some traveling funds and then steal another one to go back home when the coast was clear. And sometimes he did it just because stealing horses was fun.

Sile stole things even when he had money in his pocket to pay for them, which was often because he was very good at what he did. But hey, what would be the fun of acquiring something the way most other people did, simply by paying for it?

His most peculiar acquisition has to be the enslaved man he purloined while on a horse-stealing trip through Kentucky. He never intended to keep the man and could have sold him. Instead, he released his victim in the free state of Ohio. This wasn't a political move based on a moral objection to slavery. Anyone who knew Sile Doty would agree that he was completely unencumbered by morals of any kind. He stole another human being because he saw him standing there ripe for the plucking. Any political views he held on the subject of slavery he kept to himself. This was nothing more than a chance to steal something he had never stolen before, and he couldn't resist the temptation. Another notch on the bedpost, so to speak.

He was jailed many times over the course of his career, thus having ample opportunities to sharpen his escape and jailbreaking skills. Even so, he actually had to serve a few sentences. He called Michigan's Jackson prison home on a few occasions and once even had two years taken off one of his sentences there—for good behavior. Too bad his behavior wasn't that good outside of jail.

He never retired and was still stealing merrily well into his seventies. He died at the home of his son George in Reading, Michigan, on March 15, 1876. His autobiography, *The Life of Sile Doty, the Most Noted Thief and Daring Burglar of His Time*, was published four years after his death. The book itself was as self-aggrandizing as its title and obviously the work of man who was proud of his nefarious accomplishments. His family definitely didn't share that pride and tried unsuccessfully to block the book's publication. They even claimed that he hadn't written it and that the information therein was false. Nice try, but it didn't work.

THOSE BANK ROBBING
BIDWELL BOYS

All my life I wanted to be a bank robber. Carry a gun. Wear a mask.
Now that it's happened, I guess I'm just about the best bank robber they ever had.
And I sure am happy.
—John Dillinger

George Bidwell was born in New York probably in 1835, the eldest of a clan that would number seven. Austin was the youngest. Their parents were strict Methodists, so the children were not allowed to play on Sunday. The senior Bidwells considered everything done in this life as simply preparation for the afterlife. The younger generation was more interested in making the most of their life on earth—by whatever means presented themselves.

The brothers loved their father, but Austin especially thought him naïve. One reason was his father's belief that his kids had received a good education courtesy of the New York Brooklyn Public Schools. Austin found that amusing, never believing for a minute that a nodding acquaintance with algebra and a modest sampling of the literary greats prepared one for a successful life, especially the life he would live. The family eventually moved to a farm in the Muskegon area on Mona Lake.

Their father was not a particularly astute businessman, so although he preferred being the owner of the business rather than the employee, he frequently suffered failures. When George was only twelve, one of those reversals occurred, and the dutiful son stepped up and opened a street stand where he sold a variety of items; he did it successfully enough to support the family. He even managed to set aside enough money to buy a grocery business in Grand Rapids and run it with his father. They did well until about 1854, when the business failed. Though only nineteen, George again proved his responsibility by selling jewelry and other personal possessions to pay off the debt.

A few years later, George decided that the time had come to move to New York and try his luck there. Once again he quickly found success, and once again, it was in a grocery business—this time as a marketing agent. While in New York, he met and married Martha Anna Brewer. They had two children, daughter Helen Elaine and son Howard.

All went well with his job until a dispute arose over a receipt for a ten-dollar purchase. George was accused of embezzlement and jailed. As soon as he appeared before the magistrate, the misunderstanding was cleared up and he was released. But it was too late. Rumor and innuendo have probably ruined almost as many careers as actual crime, and George fell victim. George Bidwell was done in New York.

He did, however, have a talent for landing on his feet, and this time would be no exception. With no job, he turned his attention elsewhere and invented a steam kettle that brought in a few thousand dollars. This was not a fortune, but it was a windfall that provided the wherewithal to pull up stakes and start a wholesale confectionery business in Toronto in the Canadian province of Ottawa.

There, a chance encounter would turn his life in yet another direction. With his wife and family still in New York, George needed something to do in the evenings, and he visited a few billiard parlors. One night, he struck up a conversation with Frank Kibbe, who confided that he had a rather large problem. He was owed $1,000 but was unable to claim the money because it would alert his creditors. He offered George $500 to pick up his bounty.

George agreed and in so doing proved to Kibbe that he could be trusted. That's when Kibbe persuaded George to accompany him to Providence, Rhode Island, where they began a swindling operation; by gradually gaining the confidence of wholesalers, they soon had accumulated a large amount of stock. Next Kibbe sent George to New York to do business for the firm.

After that trip, con artist George realized that he had gone into business with another con artist. During his absence, Kibbe had sold all the stock at a discount and absconded with $21,000. George tracked him down in Buffalo, and his former partner reluctantly paid up. Kibbe learned the hard way that

Old Bailey, the London court where the Bidwell brothers and their accomplices were tried and convicted. *Library of Congress.*

it was a bad decision to try conning another con man rather than finding a more gullible victim.

It wasn't that there was anything fundamentally wrong with the local banks, but George and Austin Bidwell, with two accomplices George McDonald and Edwin Noyes, wanted to set their sights higher. They figured if you're going to be robbers, you might as well rob the best. To them, that meant the Bank of England, known in London as the Grand Old Lady of Threadneedle Street.

"As safe as the Bank of England" folks once said. That was before Muskegon's Bidwell brothers managed to break through the impenetrable layers of the venerable bank's security for a take of what would be upward of $5 million in today's numbers. No one had done it before, and no one has done it since.

They knew that rushing in with blazing guns would only land them in jail. They knew, too, that the Tower of London prison wasn't known for treating prisoners kindly, which didn't really matter because the Tower was usually nothing more than a brief stop on the way to the gallows. Those wigged and powdered judges at Old Bailey seemed to particularly enjoy issuing hanging sentences for criminal acts that included the use of firearms—sometimes for crimes as minor as stealing a loaf of bread.

No, an armed robbery was a risk best not taken. Instead, they devised a clever scam using forgeries to create false credentials enabling them to withdraw a fortune with relative ease. More importantly, they would be long gone when the theft was discovered. And had they not made the tiniest of mistakes, it would have worked.

In the 1800s, when the crime occurred, that was quite a feat. White-collar crime at that time consisted mainly of employees embezzling from their employers. Computers, the weapon of choice today, were unheard of, so the brothers were forced to do the deed through actual face-to-face interactions.

In 1849, George was sixteen and working with his father, Austin Burnham Bidwell, in a Grand Rapids confectionery shop the two had started. Business was brisk for a good six years but ultimately failed. George left Michigan for New York City, where for a time he sold wholesale groceries. Always one to look after his family, he sent for them. His father had since moved to Muskegon, where he was having a hard time making ends meet.

George Bidwell met George McDonald while working in New York. McDonald was Harvard educated, but that probably wasn't where he had learned his current occupation: forgery. The two Georges became partners and were doing quite well. Unfortunately, their way to success had meant turning from the straight and narrow to what they called the "Primrose Way," a term borrowed from William Shakespeare, who used it as a polite way to describe the road to hell in his play *Macbeth*.

The other accomplice was Edwin Noyes Hills, who was known as Ed Noyes. Each player had a role to fill. George Bidwell was the mastermind. Austin was the confidence man, a natural for the position, as the *Chicago Tribune* referred to him as an ingenious scoundrel. Austin and Noyes met years earlier as schoolmates. Noyes was the bagman. George McDonald was the forger.

Eventually, it seemed that the time had come to move on to even bigger things in England and continental Europe. Austin had traveled Europe extensively, handling illegal transfers of financial papers for men he had met while working in various capacities on New York's Wall Street. The shenanigans occurred during Boss Tweed's Tamany Hall era of corruption.

Always thinking proactively, George Bidwell set his younger brother Austin up in France. It seemed a smart move to have someone who had no part at all in the forgeries on hand to deal with authorities if and when the need arose. George also needed Austin in Paris to obtain a bill of exchange from Rothschild and Sons, then the top financial house in Europe. Austin married Jeannie Devereaux while in living in Paris. The Devereauxs were living in a state of genteel poverty near the Marble Arch.

Jeannie's mother wisely suspected that her daughter's husband-to-be was not all he pretended and tried in vain to stop the marriage. Austin later said that just as he was stepping into a taxi with his intended, along came her mama, who gave her what he described as a fearful pounding. When Mama realized that she could not stop the young lovers, she did the decent thing and attended but fainted during the ceremony.

Jeannie was about twenty at the time and naïve. When she heard about the Bank of England theft after the fact, she reacted with shock, saying, "Someone has stolen money from the Bank of England. Who would have the audacity? He should get a whipping." Austin later said that it was probably some rich guys who only did it for the thrill. For once, Austin told the truth.

Mama Devereaux won in the end. When she heard that the authorities were looking for a Mr. Horton, as Austin was then calling himself, and that he had been seen in the company of a beautiful young woman with golden hair, she immediately connected the dots and ratted him out. Anthony Trollope's *The Way We Live Now* was reportedly based on the Bidwells' crimes.

Before all that, the four thieves had to work on their plan. They turned their attention to creating the illusion of wealth and respectability. The first order of business was to establish credit by ordering large wardrobes of hand-tailored clothing. Austin did this under an assumed name, F.A. Warren. Just to make sure he appeared credible, he doubled the order. The tailor, a Bank of England client, had been carefully chosen to be their entrée into establishing accounts at the Bank of England. He did this by asking the tailor to hold on to a large sum of money for him. The tailor refused and offered instead to introduce "Mr. Warren" to his banker. This, too, was planned in advance, as the Bank of England only accepted clientele known to the management.

Of course, their plan to cheat the venerable institution was too large an undertaking to do without adequate preparation. So they practiced around the continent by swindling smaller banks in other European countries. Practice makes perfect, so after becoming very good at what they did, they pulled off the bigger heist.

What stopped them in the end was the failure to date one of their forged deposits. The bank went to the issuer for the missing date. It was the first the issuer had seen of the document. Oops! The perfect crime went belly-up due to a lack of attention to detail.

The Bank of England put a team of twenty Pinkerton detectives on the case. George led them on a convoluted path to Wales, Ireland and Scotland before being captured back in London by a private detective, James McKelvie, a Pinkerton operative. Captain John Curtin found Austin in Havana, Cuba, a short time later. The fugitive was enjoying dinner with his wife, Jeannie, and a few friends at a hacienda on the ocean. Austin escaped by jumping off the balcony but was captured a few days later.

Both Bidwells, along with George McDonald and Edwin Noyes, were tried in the Old Bailey court. The presiding judge was Thomas Dickson Archibald, also known as "Mr. Justice Archibald." They were charged with forging numerous bills of exchange with intent to steal from the governor and from the Bank of England. All four pleaded not guilty in a trial that went on for more than a week. More than one hundred witnesses testified, and all four were convicted and given life sentences to be served in London's Newgate Prison.

While in prison, George wrote *Forging His Chains: The Autobiography of George Bidwell*. When George was released from Newgate Prison after serving twenty years, Martha welcomed him home with open arms. She had stood by her husband during his England trial and also when he faced lesser charges along the way. Sources differ. According to the Bidwell Museum, "She was a strong, ambitious, loving individual who raised her family and held up well under the terrific pressures and embarrassment caused by the criminal acts of her husband." And her brother-in-law as well.

So maybe she welcomed him with open arms out of loyalty and affection. Another source claims that she was running a few of her own cons and wanted to learn the art from someone who was better at it than she was. The Bidwell Museum account is probably accurate, but either way, she allowed him to buy a business in her name. Martha died in 1930, outliving her husband by thirty-one years.

The Bidwells' sister, Harriett Bidwell Mott, who had been instrumental in their release from prison, had settled comfortably on what was once the family farm on Mona Lake in what is now Norton Shores. She died in 1909 in Muskegon Heights.

You would think that the spoils of their life on the "Primrose Path" would have enabled them to live out their lives in luxury. It didn't. On March 27, 1899, Austin Bidwell died of pneumonia in a cheap Butte, Montana hotel room at age fifty-five. George was with him. They were in Montana promoting Austin's book about their Bank of England adventure, *From Wall Street to Newgate via the Primrose Way: How I Became the World's Biggest*

Fraudster. Like many criminals' literary offerings, this one contains more braggadocio than remorse.

Three weeks later, George, sixty-seven, succumbed to pneumonia in the same hotel room—at least that's how the death certificate read. The undertaker believed that George's death was suicide by poison. George's estate consisted of two overcoats and a steamer trunk containing clothing, a few personal items and 130 copies of Austin's book.

FAUX ROYALS BEHAVING BADLY

The Boston Tea Party of December 16, 1773, should have proved conclusively that the citizens of this infant country were escaping a monarchy in favor of living in a democracy. Even so, there would always be a few dissidents who thought otherwise. Michigan was home to two of them.

JAMES JESSE STRANG

If I want a crown I must go and hunt it for myself.
—Rudyard Kipling

Jesse James Strang was born on May 23, 1813, in Cayuga, New York. From childhood on, he had dreamed of greatness and power and fancied himself the next Julius Caesar or Napoleon Bonaparte. Another way he thought he could begin the journey to his destiny would be to become a king. Then he would be able to acquire all that he felt entitled to. Easier said than done. By his late teens, he had come to realize that kings were either born to the job or married into it.

As a son of modest American farmers Clement and Abigail Strang, he knew that his only chance was Plan B and tried to come up with a way to marry Victoria, the thirteen-year-old girl who was the heir apparent to the English throne. Fortunately for Victoria, and also for Prince Albert, he failed. The Strang family of rural New York simply was not on the radar of any of Europe's crowned heads.

He later legally changed his name from Jesse James to James Jesse, as he believed James had a more regal ring. There had been previous kings named James, one of whom even had his name stamped on a version of the Bible, but Strang was unable to come up with even one King Jesse.

The would-be king was a mass of contradictions. He had once claimed to be an atheist but had also claimed to have been a Baptist minister. He married his first (and only legal) wife, Mary, with whom he had three children. He studied law and occasionally practiced. His legal career took him and his family to Nauvoo, Illinois, a move that forever changed his life. In Nauvoo, he met Joseph Smith, the leader of the Church of Latter-day Saints, more commonly known as Mormons. Smith baptized him into the faith and soon after was killed by a mob in Carthage, Illinois, when the Mormons were driven out of Nauvoo. Smith's brother Hyrum was also killed.

Though unfortunate in the extreme for Joseph and Hyrum Smith, James Jesse Strang pounced on what he saw as the opportunity of a lifetime. Smith had done well, no doubt about it, but with Strang's formal education coupled with his wiliness, he knew that he would do even better. He claimed that an angel had appeared to him with a message giving him the location of the six Rajah Manchou brass plates. Smith supposedly had first found the plates, but after translating them into the Book of Mormon, he had put them back in the hiding spot buried under a tree. He published the Book of Mormon in 1830. Strang also conveniently had a letter from Smith naming him as the one true prophet destined to relocate and lead the denomination's followers.

When Strang found the plates, one of them conveniently stated that there would be a forerunner (Joseph Smith) to be followed by that one true prophet. That prophet, of course, would be James Jesse Strang. From the plates, which supposedly told the story of an ancient people who were killed, Strang wrote the Book of the Law of the Lord. He also unearthed the Plates of Laban, which he claimed told the most important parts of the laws given by God to Moses. Much later, the "proof" was deemed fake, but while hundreds of "Strangites" did indeed follow him, thousands more Mormons hitched their wagons to Brigham Young's rising star and followed him to Salt Lake City, Utah.

Strang led his followers first to Voree, Wisconsin (now called Spring Prairie). The word *voree* means "garden of peace" in ancient Greek. It was only a temporary location, as he soon moved the flock to Beaver Island, Michigan, located on Lake Michigan off the shore of what is now the resort

James Jesse Strang was Beaver Island's self-appointed Mormon prophet and self-crowned king.

city of Charlevoix. He found it perfect for his purposes, right down to the abundant virgin pine forests, ripe for the taking. It also looked to him like the ideal spot to establish a kingdom.

In another example of his contradictory nature, he had emphatically denounced polygamy, both verbally and in the local newspaper he wrote and published. It wasn't long before he did an about-face, not only endorsing but also practicing it. That's when he decided that plural marriages were wrong for everyone else but him. He met Elvira Field, a seventeen-year-old teacher from Charlotte, Michigan, when she came to a conference on Beaver Island and found her attractive. The attraction proved mutual, and he confided in her that after the death of their first child, Mary refused to have intimate relations with him. That was definitely not true, as she had since given birth to two more babies.

Elvira became his first polygamous wife, and he so enjoyed her company that he often had her dress in men's clothing and travel with him, posing as his private secretary, Charles J. Douglass. It was noticed by some that Charles had a particularly curvaceous body for a young man of nineteen. As a way of thumbing their noses at convention, the couple named their first child Charlie. After Elvira, he married Betsy McNutt, Sarah Wright and Sarah's sister, Phoebe Wright. They gave him a combined total of twelve children. Soon after James married Elvira, Mary took her two children and left Beaver Island forever. Polygamy has to be difficult if all the wives are not on board with it.

With his long-held desire of a kingdom reawakened, he ordered his coronation. He was assisted in that endeavor by his then friend and follower (but future enemy) George J. Adams. The coronation itself had a festive air.

His royal highness wore a long, red flannel robe trimmed with white fur and designed by Elvira and a tin crown polished to look like gold and adorned with Latter-day Saints symbols. At the time of the coronation, Adams served as prime minister and viceroy in the kingdom. Strang later excommunicated Adams for embezzlement, adultery, drunkenness and apostasy. His greatest sin, in Strang's opinion, occurred when he brought a prostitute to the island and claimed that she was his wife.

Contrary to popular belief, Strang did not proclaim himself king of Beaver Island, but rather king of the Kingdom of God on Earth. Unfortunately for him, he couldn't resist acting as if he were indeed king of the island and all who dwelled thereon. That did little to endear His Royal Highness to his not-so-loyal subjects. Along with being the one true prophet of his church, king, newspaper writer and publisher, he had his fingers in a few other pies as well. One was serving as postmaster.

President Millard Fillmore added to Strang's difficulties when he ordered Captain Charles H. McBlair of the USS *Michigan* to bring Strang to Mackinac Island, where he was charged with numerous crimes, including delaying the mail, cutting timber on public lands, counterfeiting and questionable taxation practices in the form of forced tithing of the gentile (non-Mormon) population.

The trial took place in Detroit. Strang dusted off his legal skills and acted as his own lawyer. This was a case where the one acting as his own counsel did not have a fool for a client. Although he was guilty of all charges, his polished eloquence won the case with ease. That gave him credibility among the region's gentiles, and he went on to be elected to two terms of the Michigan legislature, where he served admirably. He was intelligent and articulate, both of which made it possible to con his followers as well as serve in government. Even the worst of scoundrels have some good traits. It turned out the president was no match for the king.

Strang was killed just twelve years after Joseph Smith. Although it's likely, it was never proven that Captain McBlair or any of his officers were part of the murder plot. Strang's subjects grew weary of his heavy-handed rule and began to rebel. One of the main complainers was Thomas Bedford. Their troubles began earlier when the king had him lashed seventy-nine times for bedding another man's wife. It should come as no surprise that Bedford held a grudge. Another dispute between the two occurred when Strang ordered all women to wear garments similar to bloomers. As part of the ensuing Bloomer Rebellion, Bedford's wife refused, and her husband took her side.

As reported by the *Northern Islander* on June 20, 1856, Bedford approached another dissident, Alexander Wentworth, and they took matters into their own hands. When the steamer USS *Michigan* docked at St. James, then the largest town on Beaver Island, Captain McBlair sent a messenger, Alexander St. Barnard, to bring his majesty to the boat for a meeting. Strang agreed to meet and willingly went along. As he stepped on the bridge to the dock, Bedford (armed with a horse pistol) and Wentworth (armed with a revolver) shot him three times. The assassins fled in the same boat, indicating that the captain could easily have been part of the plot. McBlair did his duty and transported them to the authorities in Mackinac City, where they were arrested.

Two other members of the assassins' group were an itinerant daguerreotypist, con artist and blackmailer calling himself "Dr. Atkyn" and Hezekiah McCullough. McCulloch had once been part of the royal inner circle and had served as viceroy and prime minister before humiliating himself with public drunkenness. He was considered the chief conspirator, although he didn't fire a weapon.

The theory that McBlair may have been involved is supported by the facts that the captain had told the governor he suspected Strang of committing robbery and fraud by overstating the island's population, that he lured Strang to the ship and that he observed the assassination and did nothing to stop it. Despite all that, no formal investigation ever took place.

After spending less than an hour in jail, the killers were ordered to pay court costs and then released. Neither was ever charged with the murder, and they returned home to a hero's welcome. The Mormons were then given twenty-four hours to leave Beaver Island. More than 300 Mormons were forced to board the steamer *Buckeye State* and dropped off at various ports along Lake Michigan, including Chicago, Racine, Milwaukee and Green Bay. Another 2,700 also left, causing renowned Michigan historian Byron S. McCutcheon to call July 5, 1856, the most disgraceful day in Michigan history.

That clearly shows the prejudice Mormons faced. The island's gentiles already resented the Mormons for crowning a king and practicing polygamy. They also thought they were murderers and thieves and were believed to damage lighthouses to cause shipwrecks and then plunder the destroyed ships. They stole horses, destroyed fishing nets and committed acts of piracy on the shores of Lake Michigan.

All this was reported on a regular basis by D.C. Leach in the *Grand Traverse Herald*. There was just one problem. Leach hated the Mormons, so his accounts were at best exaggerated and at worst totally fabricated. Strang defended his flock by saying that no Mormon was ever convicted of any of those alleged crimes.

Though mortally wounded, Strang clung to life and, with two of his wives, Betsey and Phoebe, traveled back to Voree, Wisconsin, where he died four days later on July 9, 1856, at age forty-three. Four of his wives were pregnant at the time of his death.

Several hundred Strangite Mormons still exist today, mostly scattered about in the Midwest, although none remains on Beaver Island.

ALBERT MOLITOR

I'll handle this mob of peasants.
—Albert Molitor

The state's other would-be king was rumored to have half a royal pedigree. But because he was born on the wrong side of the blanket, his father, King Wilhelm (now referred to as William I) of Wurtemberg, never acknowledged the son his mistress bore. Although the king had no intention of ever marrying Franziske Amalia Schmid, called Fanny, he felt enough responsibility toward the child that he found a sea captain named Josef Leander Christian von Molitor and paid him handsomely to marry Fanny. Captain Molitor proved to be a good husband and father. He made sure that young Albert received a good education.

According to the story, Albert's mother served as a lady-in-waiting to King Wilhelm's wife, where she had caught the monarch's eye. The boy proved to be an excellent student and later found work as an engineer. It was a good job while it lasted, but unfortunately it didn't last long because he was caught copying plans of the Uhlan Fortress with the intent of turning them over to the Austrian government. Albert Molitor was arrested and tried for treason.

As stories go, it has all the elements of a good one: romance, political intrigue and adventure. The only problem is that it is only a story, one that was thoroughly debunked by Mark Thompson, who in 2022 retired as the director of the Presque Isle County Historical Museum. Before his retirement, Thompson authored *Molitor: The Murder of a Northern Michigan King.*

The only truth in the tale is that Albert Molitor did commit the act of treason, but again, according to Thompson, it was more likely about the fortress of Ulm, located on the Danube River. Either way, that is how Molitor eventually found his way to Michigan. He was found guilty and given the choice of prison or leaving Germany. It was a no-brainer and a lucky break, as treason was usually punished by hanging or decapitation, depending on the country one chose to betray.

Author Thompson had his work cut out for him when he began untangling the mass of misinformation surrounding the life of Albert Molitor. It would appear that the only things he could be absolutely certain of was that Molitor was born in 1842 and died in 1875. Nearly everything else that was said to have happened in between those momentous events was pure guesswork or outright fabrication.

Molitor was born in Wurttemberg, the capital of Stuttgart bordering Bavaria. While King William may have fathered an impressive array of bastards, Albert Molitor was not one of them. And although he was definitely not the illegitimate son of the reigning king, his birth was not quite scandal-free. His father, Josef Leander Christian von Molitor, was still married to his first wife, Johanne Koehler Molitor, at the time of Albert's conception. In those days, marriages and divorces required government permission.

Things moved fast as soon as the Finance Ministry granted Josef permission for both. Albert Molitor's parents were married in Evangelical Lutheran Church in Leonhardt, a Stuttgart suburb, when he was just two weeks old, so he did grow up in a two-parent household. It's even possible that his mother worked in the palace, but if she did it would have been as a maid or, if she had the skills, a seamstress. She would not have been a lady-in-waiting, as those positions were given to women of higher birth. Fanny's father was Georg Mattaus Schmid, a respected sculptor, but still a far cry from the noble class.

Young Albert did receive a good education, most likely in a German military academy, and after school found work as a draftsman. When caught copying documents to pass on to Austria, he was given the choice to go to prison or leave the country.

He chose to seek his destiny elsewhere and immigrated to the United States, where he served in the military during the Civil War. After receiving what amounted to a dishonorable discharge, he found work with the government as a surveyor. The survey was done in part to develop navigation charts to later aid in the development of lake commerce. That would take the form of dredging, as well as building locks and establishing lighthouses.

He married Lucille L. Goodell in Detroit on October 28, 1864. The couple had twin sons, Edward and Frederic Albert, born on April 21, 1868, in Detroit. He also bought his first property in the Rogers City area in 1867.

It was an island of a little more than three acres in Ocqueoc Lake located in the northern part of Presque Island County. That was how he met William Rogers, the founder of Rogers City and a man with whom he would later form a business partnership. Molitor's education enabled him to become an astute businessman and community leader in his adopted home. He became a business partner of Rogers's and eventually set himself up as the ruler of Presque Isle in Rogers City.

He has been described as a despot who only treated those he deemed his superiors or equals with courtesy. It would also be fair to say that he considered few to be equals and fewer still his superiors. His size alone made him intimidating. His sister Caroline's husband, Henry Clothier, described him as "large and exceedingly stout." Something of a bully, he also dominated all who would allow it and had a naturally cruel disposition.

Eventually, rumors that Molitor had blood ties to German royalty and had maybe even been fathered by a king began circulating in Michigan. He neither confirmed nor denied the stories. He had to have known the truth of his parentage, so it's likely that he simply wanted the cachet of having other people believe the rumors of his elevated status.

Like James Jesse Strang, Albert Molitor was killed by committee. Sixteen years after his murder, the thirteen perpetrators were finally arrested and charged. William Repke, one of those responsible, learned he was terminally ill and felt a need to clear his conscience. The resulting confession included the names of his co-conspirators. It was another two years before the trials were conducted.

Some thought that womanizing was the reason for the murder. His wife, Lucille, divorced him on the grounds of infidelity, although other reports of his skirt chasing may have been exaggerated. August Barabas, one of the men involved in the murder, claimed that he wanted to kill Molitor because he had "outraged" his wife—a polite way of saying that he had taken indecent liberties with her. It isn't known if she willingly participated in the "outrage" in question.

As Thompson states, Molitor could have had one indiscretion or one hundred. He had numerous detractors, all of whom would be quick to believe any and all accusations. One newspaper reported that "women visited him at his castle-like house built high on a hill for immoral purposes." He would keep them there for a few days until he tired of them. That story is also discredited, as the man who acted like a king actually lived in an apartment above his business, a dwelling that because of his wealth was no doubt nicely appointed but in no way could be described as palatial. Also, if a woman went missing for a few days, her absence would most likely have been noticed and commented on.

Excessive taxation is another possible motive. Because he and his cronies held all the positions of power in town, it's easy to see where that power could have been abused. The word *cronies* is a bit of a misnomer, in fairness, as many simply went along with what he wanted out of fear of repercussions.

It's also known that he grossly overcharged for the construction of Rogers City's first public school building. And he enacted a tax increase for the express purpose of building new roads. Local citizens accused him of keeping the money, a logical assumption because the roads in question were never built.

True, he was the most hated man in town, but a lot of towns have one of those. Most manage to get through life without being murdered. The hatred came primarily because he set himself up as the king of Presque Isle and acted accordingly.

Often it was Molitor's own words that caused the hatred. He told a reporter from the Detroit *Evening News*, "Do as I tell you and you will get along alright, if not you will be sorry for it. I am King of Presque Isle County."

He went even further according to one of his enemies. When it was diplomatically suggested that he had made an error, he puffed out his chest and replied, "Well I never make mistakes and I want you to understand that I am Jesus Christ." To say there was no end to his inflated opinion of himself would be understatement in the extreme.

One story perfectly demonstrates his attitude of superiority. A group of detractors went to the building where he worked and lived. They stood in front of the door barring his entrance and demanded to see his financial records. He refused—maybe because the paperwork would prove his malfeasance or maybe there was no paperwork and he kept everything in his head.

Either way, it was time for his dinner, and he refused to be deterred. He ordered his associates to bring a table and chair to where he stood and to bring his food. As he sat down to eat, he said, "I'll handle this mob of peasants."

While Molitor was not an illegitimate child (despite rumors to the contrary), he did father one. J. Paul Mayer, a cofounder of Rogers City and former partner of Molitor's, testified that Molitor had accused an unnamed woman who had worked as his housekeeper of larceny. She in turn accused him of seducing her. She was kidnapped and arrested and along with her daughter placed on train out of town. Mayer said that he rescued her, and she ended up in Detroit, where her daughter later died of consumption. Albert Molitor was the child's father.

In 1897, the parole board visited Rogers City to consider pardons for four of Molitor's killers: Grossman, Fuhrmann, Jacobs and Vogler. Author Thompson reported their opinions of Molitor's character:

> *To his equals he was courteous and companionable, but to those he deemed his inferiors, he was a despot. For years there was no one in the community who dared to oppose him or provoke him to anger. He compelled all to be subservient to him and would not pay money for labor nor for what he bought of his homesteaders and compelled the people to depend on him for the necessities of life. He was violent in temper, abusive in language, and cruel in his treatment of those around him. He played well the role of lord and master and seemed to regard these people as slaves; and he became known as the "King of Presque Isle" and the "Royal Bastard," it being claimed that he was the illegitimate son of the King of Wertemberg [sic] by a maid of honor to the queen.*

This quote refers to the king's mistress and Molitor's rumored mother as a maid of honor to the queen, a term meaning she was a lady-in-waiting to the queen, not an honorary participant in the queen's wedding. People still believed him to be born of royalty. It also implies that the murderers should be pardoned because their victim was not a very nice person.

Like with Michigan's only other king, James Jesse Strang, Molitor's demise was a direct result of his heavy-handed rule and questionable policies. Both men were assassinated by committees of citizens fed up with being forced to humor their royal pretensions.

PIRACY ON THE GREAT LAKES

Pirates did not store all their treasures in treasure chests and then bury them and draw maps. That's the movie invention. In reality, they spent their money as fast as they could steal it because they knew they were living on borrowed time.
—*Robert Kurson*

JOHN "CALICO JACK" RACKHAM

Pirate John Rackham was known as "Calico Jack" because of his colorful calico clothing. Rackham was born in Britain on December 26, 1682. Though English by birth, he was a Caribbean Islander by choice, as that was his preferred pirating venue. He especially liked working the waters around Jamaica and Cuba. He did extend his reach to the Great Lakes, specifically the waters around the Upper Peninsula, when he realized how easy it was to separate lumbermen from their cash or, better yet, steal from their ships loaded with the area's virgin timber. While there, he stole everything from unguarded cash boxes to lumber, fish and furs. He stole the furs from Canadian fur traders, again preferring to steal boats already loaded with salable booty. He accomplished this by hiding in darkness until the logger, fisherman or fur trapper was away from his vessel, then he boldly sailed away.

Rackham broke into the pirating game when he served on the *Ranger*, a ship owned by Charles Vane, and rose to rank of quartermaster. In

November 1718, Vane, Rackham and crew of close to one hundred men encountered an armed French warship. Captain Vane decided to run, not fight. Rackham and most of the crew disagreed and later removed him as captain. The crew voted for Rackham to take over as captain. The ship sailed away under Rackham's command. Rackham was not all bad, however, and gave Vane and his fifteen or so loyal supporters the second vessel in the fleet, along with ammunition and enough other supplies to safely continue their voyage—or as safe as possible during the decidedly unsafe Golden Age of Piracy.

About one month later, Rackham captured the merchant ship *Kingston* complete with cargo. The merchants who owned the cargo were not going to take that lying down and hired a squad of bounty hunters to chase him down. They found and seized the purloined ship just south of Cuba. What they didn't realize was that Rackham and most of his crew were ashore.

In 1722, Captain Charles Johnson wrote a book, *General History of Pyrates*, relating a story about Rackham and crew spending time in Cuba having their sloop refitted when a Spanish warship patrolling the coast came into the harbor with an English sloop they had seized. They saw Rackham's ship, but low tide prevented them from getting to it. Later, under cover of darkness, he rowed to the captured English vessel and fought off the Spanish guards. As dawn broke, the warship crew blasted Rackham's ship, not knowing that it was unoccupied. As they blasted away, Rackham and his men sailed by in their newest possession, the English vessel.

Rackham was known for his skill in using politics and cunning when he found himself in trouble. When Jamaican governor Woodes Rogers tried him for piracy on the high seas, Rackham admitted his guilt but claimed that Vane had forced him into piracy. He asked for a royal pardon. Because Rogers hated Vane, the pardon was granted but later rescinded.

He is also believed to be the first to allow women to be members of his crew. Anne Bonny fell in love with Jack, and he with her. The only thing standing in their way was her inconvenient husband, James Bonny, who worked for Governor Rogers. The governor learned of the affair and ordered that Anne be flogged for adultery. A gentleman, at least in this instance, Rackham offered to buy his lady love's divorce. James Bonny refused. Left with no other choice, the star-crossed lovers managed to sail away in a sloop "borrowed" from John Ham. Supposedly they married, but it isn't known if she bothered to divorce her first husband.

Like other pirates, Rackham sometimes kept the sailors working on vessels he conquered. Anne Bonny befriended one of those sailors. A jealous Calico

Jack confronted the offender. The man in question turned out not to be a man at all; it was Mary Read, a woman who had gained employment by pretending to be a man. She was a good sailor, so when he discovered her true identity, he kept her on.

All good things come to an end. In October 1720, Captain Jonathan Barnet, who had been hunting Calico Jack, managed to capture him by disabling his ship with cannon fire. The men, who were all drunk, hid below deck, while Anne Bonny and Mary Read held firm and fought to the end.

Calico Jack Rackham and his crew were sentenced to death. Anne's response begs the question of what he ever saw in her. For sure, it wasn't her warmth or compassion. "I'm sorry to see you here, but if you had fought like a man, you needn't be hanged like a dog," she told him when she visited him in prison after he decided to surrender to pirate hunters instead of fighting them.

She and Mary Read were also sentenced to death, but their sentences were commuted when both said that they were pregnant. Mary died during childbirth, so she was indeed in the family way. There's no record of Anne giving birth. Although it isn't confirmed, both women are said to have claimed that Calico Jack Rackham was the father of their unborn child.

On November 28, 1720, Calico Jack Rackham was "gibbeted" in Port Royal, Jamaica. Gibbeting is an archaic punishment where the offender is hanged in a gallows-like apparatus and then left on public display as a deterrent to other would-be offenders. True, Jamaica chose an extreme method of execution and "deterrence," but no more so than medieval London, where decapitated heads were impaled on stakes and then displayed on London Bridge. Before being displayed, the heads were washed and the hair and beards fluffed and buffed in the belief that cleaning them up made them less ghoulish. It probably didn't.

Rackham's execution occurred on an islet near the Port Royal Harbor today called Rackham's Cay. He was only thirty-eight, and although his life had been decidedly short, it was crammed with adventure in the Golden Age of Piracy. As pirates go, Calico Jack was not particularly successful and would have been long forgotten. He secured his place in history by being the first to employ female crew members and his first use of the Jolly Roger flag with its iconic skull and crossbones.

DAN SEAVEY

Captain Roarin' Dan Seavey was the area's most prolific and best-known pirate, but many of the accusations against him remain undocumented. He never drew attention to himself by playing the role of the stereotypical pirate. He wasn't known to have ever kept a parrot, worn an eyepatch, made anyone walk a plank or said goofy things like "shiver me timbers."

The bottle of rum? Probably, but in general, he drank whatever was at hand and in awe-inspiring quantities. Roarin' Dan is today commercially associated with rum, as the Great Lakes Distillery's product list includes Roarin' Dan Rum, a maple-flavored drink with Seavey's image on the bottle.

Seavey was born in Portland, Maine, on March 23, 1865. Despite later living in both Michigan and Wisconsin, he never lost his distinctive Down East twang. He kept busy, as evidenced by a long list of occupations (on both sides of the law) he held over the years. One of the legitimate jobs was serving as a lawman—U.S. deputy marshal in the Bureau of Indian Affairs. Other non-criminal ventures he dabbled in over the years included fisherman, trapper, logger and tavern keeper, along with his stints as sailor, prospector and prizefighter. His seamier roles included poacher, thief, bootlegger, smuggler, brothel operator and, oh yes, pirate.

The son of a schooner captain, he chose a seafaring life for himself at a young age and left home at around thirteen to work on a tramp steamer, forerunner of the Merchant Marine. He's also known to have served honorably in the U.S. Navy for three years. It was following his discharge from the navy that he became a deputy marshal.

His first marriage was to Mary Plumley, with whom he had two daughters, Harriet and Josephine. The marriage was doomed from the start because Dan was too restless to play the role of dutiful husband. He proved that when he joined the tens of thousands of dreamers and schemers tempted by gold in the Yukon Territory and Alaska. Like most, he came home with nothing more than memories of a grand adventure. That probably meant less to him than most of the others, as his whole life was one grand adventure.

When Mary found him after his return, he let her know that he had no intention of going home with her—ever. For him, it not just over—it was as if it had never happened. When he married the second time, this time to Zilda Bisner in Escanaba, Michigan, it appears that he did so without bothering to first get a divorce from Mary. The marriage to Zilda lasted only four years before she not only divorced him but also claimed he had beaten and threatened her life on a fairly regular basis. Seavey's third marriage, to another Upper Peninsula woman, Annie Bradley, was by all accounts a happy one and lasted until her death in 1928 at age fifty.

It is well known that he enjoyed taking part in a good fight, and those who knew him well advised keeping a safe distance away from Roarin' Dan, especially when Dan was roarin' drunk—and that was most of the time. Even when he wasn't drunk, he would be an intimidating opponent, as he was a bit over six-foot-four and weighed in at a whopping 250 pounds. He was described as rough, tough and hard to kill, leaving one to wonder how many had tried and failed. Had Mary Plumley Seavey or Zilda Bisner Seavey tried, it would be understandable, maybe even justifiable.

Even during his brief tenure as a lawman, he made no effort at subduing the pleasure he derived from barroom brawling or barroom imbibing. In one famous though probably exaggerated fight, he tracked a liquor smuggler to Nubinway in Michigan's Upper Peninsula. The outlaw had made the mistake of bragging that no lawman would ever best him in hand-to-hand combat.

There may have been lawmen who could have resisted that challenge, but Seavey was not one of them. It was said that they were pretty well matched, and the altercation went on for hours, until Seavey bested his opponent by pinning him under a piano, reportedly to hold him in place while he went for a drink. The outlaw was immediately treated for his resulting injuries but perished during the night. Marshal Seavey telegraphed a terse report to his superiors: "Outlaw expired while resisting arrest." He was never charged with his role in the outlaw's expiration.

He did engage in pirating to some extent and was suspected of "moon cussing," the practice of using fake lights on the shoreline to cause shipwrecks on the coast that could later be plundered. He was believed to seek out larger cargoes of alcohol or venison, both of which could be sold at a good profit. The alcohol shipments were probably also good for replenishing his own stock. The large cannon prominently displayed on his deck probably discouraged anyone from trying to stop him.

Seavey was better known for turning his ship into a casino or even a brothel on occasion. The first was a good idea, as gambling on the high seas is one of the most popular activities offered on cruise ships today. Floating houses of ill repute would probably be even more popular, but if such exist, they are closely guarded secrets.

Seavey called Frankfort home for several years. While there, he managed to indulge in some illegal fish trapping and venison poaching. That was also where he based his forty-two-foot two-mast schooner, the *Wanderer*.

His one known act of piracy happened when he, along with two of his thugs, stole a smaller schooner, the *Nellie Johnson*, in Grand Haven on June 11, 1908. He met the owner, Captain R.J. McCormick, and his crew members in a local tavern and plied them with liquor. If they thought they could match Dan Seavey drink for drink, they were badly mistaken. He proceeded to drink them under the table. As soon as he was sure they would put up no resistance, he sailed away in the *Nellie Johnson*. He headed first for Chicago and its extensive black market, where he expected he could easily sell the cargo of purloined cedar posts. When that failed, he returned to his home port, Frankfort. That was Seavey's only verifiable pirating adventure. He was the only man ever formally charged with piracy on the Great Lakes.

Authorities had immediately given chase, and in a few weeks, the U.S. Revenue Cutter Service tracked him down in Frankfort. They found McCormick's boat hidden in a nearby river. On June 30, he was arrested and charged with piracy, later reduced to mutiny and sedition, the unauthorized removal of a vessel on which he had once been a seaman. For reasons unknown, the charges were dropped.

There are several possible reasons. One, he had a corrupt lawyer who managed to bribe or somehow persuade the court to stop pursuing the matter. Another theory is that Captain McCormick failed to show up at the trial, or that McCormick simply decided to drop the charges. Seavey said he won the *Nellie Johnson* from McCormick in a bet. He stuck with that story for the rest of his life. For whatever reason, Michigan's most infamous pirate walked away a free man.

Toward the end of his life, Seavey had a total and unexpected character reversal. He found religion and was often seen carrying a Bible. It is also believed that he reconnected with his second wife, Zilda. If that is true, she obviously no longer considered him a threat. He lived with his daughter Josephine and son-in-law Ernest Beauchamp in Peshtigo, Wisconsin, and later in a Peshtigo nursing home, where he died in 1949 at age eighty-four. His was buried in Marinette, also in Wisconsin.

Seavey gained international fame when he was featured as a merchant vessel captain in the season 12 episode of the *Murdoch Mysteries* television series, a fictional show based in Toronto, Canada. His character was portrayed by actor Hugh Thompson.

HE WENT OUT TO LUNCH AND WAS NEVER SEEN AGAIN

I may have my faults, but being wrong ain't one of them.
—Jimmy Hoffa

One problem with hobnobbing with organized crime is that if your enemies don't kill you, it's quite possible your friends will. It doesn't really matter, though, because either way you're dead. In Jimmy Hoffa's case, it isn't yet known who did the deed, but it's assumed that someone did—and it's likely we'll never know who that someone was.

Jimmy Hoffa's birth in Brazil, Indiana, on Valentine's Day 1925 came as a surprise, and the small town's doctor may well have been the most surprised of all. He had insisted throughout her pregnancy that his mother, Viola, wasn't pregnant at all, but rather was suffering from a rapidly growing abdominal tumor. Since pregnancy is a rather easy condition to diagnose, it is surprising that Viola didn't seek a second opinion. She named the child James Riddle (using her maiden name).

His father had been a coal miner and died of coal dust inhalation when Jimmy was only seven. Viola did her best to remain in Indiana to raise her two sons and two daughters. Eventually, when Jimmy was eleven, she moved the family to Detroit, where she worked multiple jobs before landing a better-paying one at the Fleetwood Fisher Body Plant. His mother's struggles taught him, by example, the value of a strong work ethic. He became a workaholic and a wealthy one. Viola was known for having a hardness, even a mean streak, a trait that may well have been a result of the struggles she had endured in her early life.

A strong desire to contribute to the family income propelled him drop out of school. Sources vary, but it was probably just before, during or just after ninth grade. He worked odd jobs and brought home whatever money he could, and by the time he was nineteen, he had a real job in a local Kroger store.

That led to the "Strawberry Incident," where he had his first taste of how advantageous union membership might be. It was an eye opener, and his life was forever changed. Jimmy and a handful of other young employees were hired to unload trucks as they arrived. The boys thought it unfair that they were required to wait for the trucks to arrive and that no matter how long they had to wait, they didn't receive any pay until they actually started unloading.

It was well known that strawberries have a short shelf life, especially after being transported in airless trucks. Knowing that time was of the essence, he convinced his coworkers to immediately go on strike until better pay terms could be negotiated. It was not a legitimate strike because no union was in place in the store, but management heard them out. Anything to sell those berries!

That sealed his fate, and before his next birthday rolled around, he became the leader of a local one-store union of dockworkers. Not surprisingly, it was the same Kroger where his strawberry gambit had paid off. His star quickly rose. It didn't take him long to realize the mutual benefit a close working relationship with organized crime could bring.

Along the way, he married Josephine Poszywak, a Detroit laundry worker and daughter of Polish immigrants. They met during a laundry workers strike, and Hoffa married the eighteen-year-old in Bowling Green, Ohio, in September 1937. The couple had two children: a daughter, Barbara Ann, followed by their son, James Philip.

This is when Viola's mean streak reasserted itself and caused a permanent rift in the family. Jimmy and Jo, as she was called, were a love match and totally adored each other through both the joys and the tribulations they faced during their marriage. Viola openly disliked her daughter-in-law, whom she called a foreigner, and found her completely unacceptable. Jimmy was caught in the middle, and as years went by, it was the Poszywaks, not the Hoffas, who were frequently and warmly welcomed at Jimmy and Jo's Lake Orion home.

At the time of Hoffa's meteoric rise, unions and organized crime were known to be in bed together. It isn't hyperbole to call Hoffa's rise meteoric, as he single-handedly transformed a relatively small trucker's union of seventy-five thousand members into the most powerful labor union in the world. Most of the larger unions, including the Teamsters, were scandal-ridden. That said, the members fared well under his leadership, and they loved him. One reason is that they knew he would always be on their side.

He made himself available to them, often saying, "You got a problem, call me." He meant it. They knew it and they did.

They had his back in ways he didn't always know. Supposedly, one member of his trusted inner circle, Chuckie O'Brien, once sent a package containing a severed horse's head to the *Detroit News* when the paper criticized Hoffa in print. That leaves one wondering if that real-life incident inspired the horse head found in a bed in *The Godfather*—or vice versa. O'Brien didn't kill a horse to obtain the head, as he was able to buy it from the Wayne County morgue. Who knew that such things were for sale? Or that dead horses wound up in the county morgue? Young O'Brien was so close to Hoffa that he was considered an adoptive son.

Whatever else could be said about Jimmy Hoffa, he was completely devoted to both the Teamsters and to his family. An often-told story about a fishing incident with his daughter, Barbara, demonstrates that devotion. Once, when Barbara, still in her early teens, cast her line, she accidentally hooked Jimmy's eyelid. Despite the excruciating pain, he kept his composure and never once lashed out at her. He calmly rowed back to shore and drove himself to the nearest hospital emergency room, almost fifty miles distant. Barbara was crying and saying, "I'm sorry. I'm sorry," repeatedly. "Of course you are," was all he said. Daddy knew that his little girl felt terrible and didn't want her feel any worse than she already did.

He was serving as Teamster president when he was arrested in 1964, and in two separate trials he was charged with jury tampering, attempted bribery, fraud and conspiracy. He had faced those charges before, but this time he was convicted. In all his earlier trials, he had walked free. No doubt those jury tampering charges were true, and the practice had probably saved his neck in the past. Things had changed, and not in his favor.

A few months later, misuse of union retirement funds was added to the list of charges. Five years into a thirteen-year sentence, President Richard M. Nixon commuted Hoffa's sentence to time served. But there was one unwelcome condition: Hoffa could have no business with, or influence over, the Teamsters until 1980. He was still trying to overturn that ban at the time of his disappearance.

The former union and mob coziness had lessened greatly over the years, and by the 1970s, the unions had pulled away from the mafia. By then, the two entities had different goals and were often at cross-purposes. Jimmy Hoffa was one of the old school and still had one foot in each camp.

July 30, 1975, started out like any other day. He probably kissed Jo goodbye and then left his home in the Detroit suburb of Lake Orion for a 2:00 p.m.

Teamsters leader Jimmy Hoffa, who was most likely killed by the Detroit mob. *Walter Ruether Library at Wayne State University.*

lunch meeting at Machus Red Fox (now Joe Vicari's Andiamo Restaurant) in Bloomfield Hills. The two men he was to meet, Anthony Provenzano and "Tony Jack" Giacalone, never showed. Provenzano was a labor leader with mafia ties, and Giacalone was a Detroit mafia kingpin.

Obviously there was still quite a bit of cohabitation between the Detroit mafia and organized labor, despite the latter's attempt to clean up its act. It is believed that he suspected the meeting would never happen because at that time the restaurant had a strict dress code that required men to wear coats and ties. Hoffa showed up wearing a casual shirt and trousers.

Hoffa used a pay phone to call Jo and told her that he had been stood up and would be home around 4:00 p.m. He never made it. The FBI believes he was picked up and left voluntarily between 2:45 p.m. and 2:50 p.m. in a Mercury Marquis owned by Giacolone's son, Joseph. Three other men were in the car with Joseph, one of whom was Chuckie O'Brien. Though considered a suspect in the disappearance, O'Brien was never charged. Decades later, DNA testing proved that a hair found in the car belonged to Hoffa. Both Provenzano and the elder Giacalone died in prison, but neither man's prison sentence was in any way connected to the disappearance of Jimmy Hoffa. No one has ever been charged.

Hoffa's fate isn't surprising, as he did pick up some powerful enemies along the way, not the least of which was Robert F. Kennedy, who was a relentless bulldog, constantly nipping at Hoffa's heels. That situation worsened when Bobby's brother John Fitzgerald Kennedy was elected president in 1960. One of JFK's first acts was naming his brother to the cabinet post of attorney general. That gave the bulldog teeth.

Conspiracy theorists put forth the notion that both the attorney general and the president were assassinated because their father, Joseph P. Kennedy, reneged on his promise to the mafia that the government would not interfere in union or mafia business.

As theories go, the broken promise scenario is plausible, as it is well known that the elder Kennedy was a scoundrel in his own right. Joseph Kennedy was also known to have been a bootlegger during the Prohibition era and allegedly engaged in stock market manipulation. According to Dan E. Moldea, author of *The Hoffa Wars: The Rise and Fall of Jimmy Hoffa*, Joseph Kennedy enlisted the help of his mob connections to get out the vote for JFK in both West Virginia and Illinois. It's logical to assume that he would be expected to make sure his son granted a few favors after the election. Moldea has made a career out of Jimmy Hoffa, referring to himself as "Ahab." Jimmy Hoffa was his whale.

Any man who would have his mentally ill daughter lobotomized without his wife's knowledge or consent, as Joseph Kennedy did, has definitely earned the scoundrel label. Rosemary was the elder sister of John, Robert and Edward. Joseph was concerned that Rosemary's erratic behavior would be harmful to their political aspirations. Still, it would be quite a stretch to connect the Detroit mafia to either JFK's assassin, Lee Harvey Oswald, or to Sirhan Sirhan, who killed Robert Kennedy.

The FBI's theory that Hoffa fell victim to a mafia hit is probably correct, and Oakland County probate judge Norman R. Barnard declared him dead on July 30, 1982, seven years after he went missing. Since then, it's almost become a national pastime to speculate and spread rumors about where his body is buried. No leads have ever panned out. So, what we do know now is a lot of places where Jimmy Hoffa *isn't*.

He isn't under a certain New Jersey bridge or under a certain Jersey City landfill. He isn't under Detroit's downtown Renaissance Center or under a driveway in Roseville, Michigan, or under a farm field in Livingston County. He probably wasn't thrown out of an airplane over the Great Lakes. He wasn't shot, dismembered, frozen, bagged and then dumped in the cement foundation of the new Giants Stadium. The last scenario sounds as if it could have been written by Stephen King and would be difficult if not impossible to prove conclusively.

An even grislier theory is that Hoffa was killed near the restaurant and his body then taken to Hamtramck, where it was run through a cardboard shredding machine at the Central Sanitation Service, a mob-owned garbage disposal business. The building was conveniently destroyed by fire six months after Hoffa's disappearance.

It's probably not known exactly how all those theories have been eliminated—unless those putting forth the scenarios were proven to be liars. Even so, how can something as immense as the bottoms of all the Great Lakes be ruled out in one fell swoop?

One mob attorney, Reginald "Bubba" Haupt Jr., claimed that Hoffa's final resting place is under a certain hole at the Savannah, Georgia Inn and Golf Course on Wilmington Island. The course in question was once run by Chicago mafia figure Lou Rosanova. Haupt backed up his claim by reporting that Teamsters and mobsters alike make it a point to urinate in the cup in the hole in question while playing the course. Hoffa may or may not be buried there, but Bubba was right about one thing: that behavior definitely flies in the face of proper golf etiquette.

It has also been said that Hoffa is alive and well and part of the witness protection plan or that he is hiding out in a Detroit mansion. Both scenarios are highly unlikely, as voluntarily dropping out of sight and leaving his beloved family behind just wasn't his nature. Hoffa never hid from his enemies. He much preferred facing them head on and then crushing them. Even if the second had once been true, it is likely that whoever was gunning for him would have eventually caught up him and completed the mission.

All that, of course, inevitably led to fake news stories about his body being found. One of the wackiest is that the body was found by the *Storage Wars* reality show star Barry Weiss in an abandoned storage unit he had bid on and won. The public has an ongoing fascination with the fate of the missing scoundrel.

Jo Hoffa had always been in frail health and died of multiple natural causes on September 12, 1980; she was interred at the White Rose Memorial Cemetery in Troy. Her son and daughter believe that despite the numerous physical ailments listed on the death certificate, their mother also died of a broken heart.

Jimmy Hoffa may have been a high school dropout, but he made sure his children grew up knowing the value of a good education. Barbara Ann Hoffa Crancer, born in 1938, became a respected attorney and judge in St. Louis, Missouri, where she is now retired. After graduating from Albion College, she received her juris doctor degree from the Washington University of Law in St. Louis She had a private practice before being appointed to several judicial positions, the last being assistant attorney general to Chris Koster, attorney general of Missouri. Crancer spent about twenty years working closely with the FBI and trying without success to uncover the truth about what had really happened to her father. She is convinced that the truth will never be known, as all the original suspects and people who may have had information at the time have probably died.

James Phillip Hoffa, born in 1941, also became an attorney and, like his father, became president of the Teamsters, where he served five consecutive five-year terms. Unlike his infamous father, the younger Hoffa spent that time working tirelessly to fight union corruption everywhere it tried to raise its ugly head. While growing up, he often attended International Brotherhood of Teamsters meetings with his dad and became a member himself in 1959 at age eighteen. He received his first degree from Michigan State University and followed that up with a Bachelor of Law degree from the University of Michigan Law School. He served as an attorney for the IBT for thirty-five years and always advocated for fair trade and worker safety.

FALLING FROM GRACE

THE RISE AND FALL OF JIM BAKKER

Why should I apologize because God throws in crystal chandeliers,
mahogany floors and the best construction in the world?
—Jim Bakker

Why indeed? Maybe because it wasn't God who provided all those lovely accoutrements. They were provided by gullible viewers who sent money they believed would be used to spread the Gospel by keeping Bakker's ministry on the air. It was never their intention to furnish Castle Bakker.

Televangelist James Orsen Bakker entered this world in Muskegon, Michigan, on January 2, 1940, the youngest of four children born to Raleigh and Furnia Bakker. It could be said that Jim got his ability to spin the truth into whatever he wanted it to be from Raleigh. Shortly after Jim's public disgrace, Raleigh said that his son was the most popular man in America. Infamous, yes. Popular, no.

The family belonged to the Assembly of God church, a denomination with Pentecostal beliefs. Those beliefs often included the ability to speak in tongues, and they were sometimes referred to by the pejorative term "Holy Rollers." The empire Jim later built was affiliated with the Assembly of God, although many saw his ministry as notably short on theology and long on showmanship. Though only an average student, he had natural gifts for selling and performing, both of which would serve him well but eventually bring him down.

With his wife, Tammy Faye, he founded a multimillion-dollar industry. Some of those millions supported the family's lavish lifestyle. Tammy Faye's numerous wigs and heavily applied makeup spawned a common joke in the late 1970s: "It seems Tammy Faye Bakker was rushed to the hospital following an accident. The first thing they did was scrape off several layers of spackling. Guess what they found? Jimmy Hoffa!"

Tammy Faye's packaging was in direct conflict to the way Jim was raised back in Muskegon. Makeup was frowned upon, and although Jim dated girls who cosmetically enhanced their appearance, he made them wash it off when they visited his family or when he and the young lady in question attended church together.

Tammy Faye was born in International Falls, Minnesota. The couple met while both were students at North Central Bible College in Minneapolis. The attraction was both mutual and instant, with the love-stricken Jim proposing marriage on the third date. Both dropped out of college. She sang and played the guitar and accordion. Her musical talents and his ability to perform brought them success early on, starting with a children's puppet show that aired on Pat Robertson's Christian Broadcasting Network. Jim even briefly hosted Robertson's popular show *The 700 Club*.

Jim Bakker used his television ministry to unlawfully raise funds that were then used for his own purposes. *Library of Congress.*

Not surprisingly, the two men soon had creative differences. Robertson had sensed an insincerity in Bakker's preaching style. The man who always behaved with the dignity he believed went with his calling probably was unable to come to terms with copious sobbing on the air as an appropriate method of raising funds.

The insincerity Pat Robertson sensed manifested itself in a letter he wrote to Bakker in September 1977 that ended with this plea: "Jim, God does not bless falsehood, and the Bible says He resists the proud. Unless you face reality and ask God's forgiveness, He is going to bring you down. God is speaking to you through things that are happening. I pray that you will get His message." To say Jim failed to get the message is understatement. That's hardly surprising, as Bakker considered himself to be a deliverer, not a receiver of messages.

From the earliest days of his career, Jim Bakker quarreled with management at his various television station enterprises. The in-fighting was always about money and control, as he could never get enough of either. One station manager wisely told him that "the talent [meaning the Bakkers] should never manage the business." A polite way of saying that the inmates shouldn't run the asylum.

Staff, especially management, seemed to come and go through a revolving door. Anyone disagreeing with Bakker or trying to rein him in soon found themselves out in the cold. Occasionally, someone was able to reason with him, like a former financial manager who convinced him that operating costs had to be cut. Jim complied by firing 60 of his 660 employees. So far, so good, but he followed up by having the board authorize a sizeable increase in his own salary. One of those frustrated managers later described him as a petulant, overstimulated child accustomed to having his way—and throwing a tantrum when he didn't.

Bakker never returned to school because he believed that appearances, not a solid base of theological knowledge, were the key to success, especially on television. He had turned down offers of Fords or Chevys in favor of Cadillacs and Lincolns. According to him, expensive clothing and luxury cars showed the world that his God was a generous God. It probably never occurred to him that people might come to wonder why God chose to shower a disproportionate amount of that generosity on the Bakker family.

Eventually, the fairy-tale marriage began showing cracks. Both camps claimed infidelity. Tammy Faye admitted that she had romantic feelings for Gary Paxton, a musician who sometimes appeared on their show and who also recorded her albums in Nashville. She was prolific and released one or two albums a year, so they did spend quite a bit of time together. Like former president Jimmy Carter, she said that she had only lusted in her heart and had never had intimate relations with Paxton. Gary Paxton categorically denied the rumors. Jim would later retaliate with Jessica Hahn. According to Hahn, Jim Bakker's lusting involved a few more body parts than just his heart. Truth be told, his heart didn't seem to have been involved at all.

Like many people who had grown up poor, Tammy often felt insecure. She chose the makeup, the wigs and the four-inch heels to feel better about herself. Adding to her insecurities was Jim's manic devotion to his latest project. He worked long hours, leaving her home alone, where she hoped against hope that some of that attention would eventually be focused on her. It didn't happen.

She was childlike in her faith, keeping up a running, if one-sided, dialogue with God about everything from her pets to the color of the carpet in her home. Tammy was quoted as saying, "If you give God $20, he'll give you back $200." That may have worked beautifully for her, but for most of the already cash-strapped victims, it simply meant twenty fewer dollars to spend on groceries.

She also had a habit of saying, "Thank you, Jesus" each time she stepped in a bubble bath. That said, any heartfelt gratitude she felt for the smaller pleasures failed to keep her from being a willing participant in her husband's greedy quest for more, more, more!

Although the couple separated briefly, they sought marriage counseling and soon reconciled, but it was too little and too late. Tammy confided in friends that she was unhappy but believed that the tenets of her faith gave her no viable options. Despite her perceived innocence, she knew how people viewed her and was even able to joke about it. When Larry King interviewed her, he asked what she wanted to be remembered for. "My eyelashes," she quipped.

Jim Bakker founded the PTL (Praise the Lord or sometimes People that Love) Club and devoted himself to convincing his viewers that the best way to praise the Lord was to send money to himself and Tammy Faye. Unfortunately, far too many believed him.

When he dreamed of a peaceful retreat that families could visit to relax and recharge their faith, he did what he always did and dreamed too big. Instead of that peaceful retreat, he created more of a "Christian Disney World" that he named Heritage USA, and operated in Fort Mill, South Carolina, part of the Charlotte Metropolitan Area, from 1978 to 1989. He was never quite satisfied and kept adding to the facility, which included a water park, a luxurious hotel and a shopping mall, among other extravagant amenities.

Always milking his enterprises to the limit, Jim began selling life memberships to Heritage USA for $1,000. Memberships include perks, one of which was that members would be guaranteed three free nights a year. Once again his unbridled enthusiasm was his undoing. Unfortunately, he was so caught up in the plan that he failed to do the math. He sold thousands, but the effort was doomed to fail when demand for the free nights greatly exceeded the supply.

Bakker referred to his viewers as partners, giving them the illusion that they were part of his ministry. One thing leading to his downfall was his habit of telling those "partners" about PTL's television ministry expanding into far-flung places like Brazil and Korea. That, of course, took money, and no one was better at fundraising than Jim Bakker. Donations poured in, but the money stayed in Fort Mill, South Carolina. It turned out that it's against the law to go on national television to collect money for one purpose and then use it for something else. Those "something elses" included adding structures to Heritage USA, houseboats and tens of thousands of dollars spent on furnishings and payments to an interior decorator.

The family, including son Jamie Charles and daughter Tammy Sue, lived a lavish lifestyle financed by, you guessed it, money taken in to support the organization, not Jim and Tammy Faye's uncontrollable extravagances. The Bakkers never had the ability to sit back and enjoy what they had accomplished. In Fort Mill, they frequently moved into a new and better house. They also had a vacation house on Lake Wiley and bought not one but two houseboats, paid for with "loans" from PTL, as well as frequent bonuses approved by the board. Their dogs dwelled in air-conditioned doghouses.

Bakker admitted to having what he called consensual sex with Jessica Hahn at least three times. In one of those encounters, he entered her hotel room clad only in white terrycloth swimming trunks. He did the deed and then, without a word, got up and walked out of the room. Slam and bam but without the proverbial "Thank you, Ma'am." At the very least, the encounter happened, although at one point she accused him of raping her. His "consensual" spin would not have saved him from any resulting scandal. Not only was it behavior unbecoming a minister, but he was also still married to Tammy Faye.

Hahn later said that it was her extreme anger at being forced to sign a false confession stating that she had, in fact, seduced him and that he was blameless. Had that been true, there was nothing to stop him from pulling a Nancy Reagan and just saying no. She claimed that she didn't want to hurt God's people. He claimed he was "set up by a female."

Hahn was smart enough to get a lawyer and threaten public exposure. The scandal would have ended the Bakker empire, and she knew it. He knew it too. She accepted a settlement of an immediate cash payout coupled with a twenty-year trust fund, the latter a brilliant move to buy her silence for at least twenty years.

Jim Bakker was well received in Charlotte, North Carolina, and the confidence that gave him helped fuel his ill-conceived notion that he was invincible and ultimately led to his downfall.

Bakker's FCC trial testimony, as well as interviews he gave and what he told his television viewers, whom he referred to as partners, can best be described as the "gospel according to Jim Bakker." Although unfavorable publicity increased at an alarming rate, Bakker's television audience continued to stand by him. He knew which buttons to push and freely talked about the accusations being thrown at him. He held on to their support by convincing them that there was no truth to the allegations, that it was all a secular liberal media's attempt to destroy Christianity. In reality, the goal was simply to hold one man responsible for his reprehensible behavior.

The eventual collapse of Bakker's house of cards was brought on in large measure by the *Charlotte Observer*, the local newspaper whose management and reporters sensed that all was not as it seemed at PTL and relentlessly exposed Jim's attempts to cover his tracks. The scope and quality of the newspaper's investigative reportage captured a 1988 Pulitzer Prize. Reporter Charles E. Shephard's comprehensive book, *Forgiven: The Rise and Fall of Jim Bakker and the PTL Ministry*, details the long and twisted path to exposing the truth.

Imprisoned after being charged and convicted of twenty-four counts of mail and wire fraud, Bakker received a sentence of forty-five years and was fined $500,000. Tammy Faye initially stood by him but chose to get a divorce while he was incarcerated. He served only five years before being paroled. Having paid his debt to society, he promptly reinvented himself.

That makeover took the form of—surprise, surprise—a new television talk show ministry called *The Jim Bakker Show*, along with a new wife. Another of Bakker's many talents seems to be the ability to land on his feet. He met Lori Beth Graham early in 1998, and they married in September of that year.

Graham was born and raised in Phoenix, Arizona, where in her early teens she gravitated to a life of hard drugs and hard living. She admitted to having had five abortions, the last one at age twenty-two. Like Bakker, Graham also married young the first time. But there was no happily-ever-after for her either. Instead, it turned out to be an abusive marriage that lasted for ten years. Near the end of the marriage, she turned her life around when she found and joined the First Assembly of God church in Phoenix.

In 1991, she became an ordained minister. All that eventually led to an interview on Jim Bakker's new show and a second marriage for them both. In the interview, she said, "I have always enjoyed ministering to women, and this live show is a prophecy come to pass to have my heart touch the hearts of women worldwide." Give the lady a high score for trying to help other women avoid the pitfalls of her own early life.

Graham is also the author of *More Than I Could Ever Ask*, described on Amazon as "the story of a woman broken and defeated who found out that dreams really can come true." In 2002, the couple cemented their marriage by adopting seven children.

After his makeover, Bakker once famously greeted an audience by saying, "You're too young to know me, and that's good."

Did Jim Bakker's new life represent redemption following a calamitous fall from grace? Not quite. It seems old habits are hard to break. While the rest of the world saw the COVID-19 pandemic as an unprecedented disaster, Jim, who just can't seem to help being Jim, saw it as an unprecedented moneymaking opportunity. He claimed that he had a cure, and of course, that cure was available only to his viewers.

Although the State of Missouri, where his show is broadcast, sued him, he didn't go to prison again. But he was made to pay $156,000 in restitution to give refunds to all who were gullible enough to actually buy the bogus product. Now he preaches about the end of the world on his show and endorses products to help people prepare for an apocalypse.

As for Tammy Faye, her life held dramatic changes too. She went on to marry Roe Messner, a family friend and contractor who had a hand in building Heritage USA, as well as other megachurches. It was he who supplied $265,000 to reach a settlement with Jessica Hahn. But like her first husband, Messner was known to straddle both sides of the law and served a twenty-seven-month prison sentence for fraud.

The couple was also forced into bankruptcy. But that wouldn't be her biggest challenge. She received a crushing colon cancer diagnosis in 1996 and underwent immediate surgery. Although the surgery was deemed a success, the cancer returned a few years later and by then had metastasized to her lungs. In 2007, eleven years after the first diagnosis, Tammy Faye Messner died of the disease she no longer had the strength to fight.

Her daughter, Tammy Sue Bakker-Chapman, was her caretaker during the last two years. Although the two had gone through the usual mother-daughter power struggles as Tammy Sue was growing up, any rifts were immediately forgotten with the cancer diagnosis. Tammy Sue rushed to her mother's side and described their pre-hospitalization night as "an orgy of junk food and all-round silliness." The younger Tammy was by then married to Douglas Chapman, a former Heritage USA hotel worker. She now lives in St. Louis and works on the current *Jim Bakker Show*.

Jim and Tammy Faye's son, Jamie Charles, also became a minister and uses the name Jay Bakker. He works in the inner city of Atlanta, Georgia, where he cofounded the Revolution Church, a ministry known for reaching out to those who no longer feel that traditional churches fulfill their needs. He married Karin Aebersold, with whom he has one child.

And Jessica Hahn, the so-called bad girl who hastened Jim Bakker's downward spiral? At the time of the disgrace, she worked as a sometime actor and sometime model. She posed nude in *Playboy* and appeared in a few adult movies.

She has put all that in the past and enjoys her current, more conservative lifestyle on a forty-five-acre California ranch with her husband, Hollywood movie stuntman Frank Lloyd. Their ranch is home to the usual critters found on a working ranch and also Jessica's special pet, a turkey named Pearl.

Decades later, the scandal still commands attention, as evidenced by Elton John's new musical, *Tammy Faye*, which opened on October 26, 2022, in London's Almeida Theatre to mixed reviews.

Benjamin Purnell's Benton Harbor Sect

The difference between a cult and a religion is that one outlasts its leader.
—*Rakesh Khurana*

Another case of a religious leader gone bad is that of Benjamin Franklin Purnell, founder, with his wife, Mary Stallard Purnell, of the Israelite House of David, a communal sect located first in Fostoria, Ohio. One of the tenets of the faith and a rule of the commune was to stay away from the dead. Public opinion forced the couple out of Ohio when they failed to attend the funeral of their sixteen-year-old daughter, Hettie, in 1903. Hettie had found work in the Fox Ammunition Factory in Fostoria and was killed on her first day on the job when the building exploded.

They moved their operations to Benton Harbor. Mary was Benjamin's second wife. He had abandoned his first wife, Angeline, and daughter, Sarah. He never divorced that first wife, so legally he was a bigamist, but in Kentucky, where the marriage took place, the fact that the bride was only fourteen meant that a divorce was not required. Yes, girls married younger in those days, but from the vantage point of time, a child abuse charge would not have been inappropriate.

Followers adhered to rules prohibiting meat, alcohol, tobacco, haircuts and shaving. Each no-no was rooted in a Bible verse. Members differed from other denominations and believed that not only the soul but also the body would live forever as soon as the expected millennium came. That belief meant that sex was also taboo, as there would no longer be a need to procreate. Marriages were permitted after the couple received Purnell's blessing, but they had to refer to each other as brother and sister. Purnell was later accused of forcing young girls into loveless marriages when outsiders began questioning what really went on in the commune.

The Benton Harbor locals had a difficult time figuring out exactly who these people were and what they stood for. Some assumed that they were Jewish, a logical mistake based on the word "Israelite" in their name. Also, their flowing hair and beards made them look like a country bumpkin version of Hasidic Jewish men.

The House of David founder embraced religion in early childhood. Following his mother's death, he went to live with his elder brother, James. His sister-in-law, Elizabeth, later said that Benjamin used the New Testament to teach himself to read. She also said that he often preached to trees on the property as if practicing for his future calling. Sometime in the 1880s, Purnell read the book *The Flying Roll*, written by James Jershom Jazreel. The eight-hundred-page book was a collection of sermons.

The sect actually traced its roots to Joanna Southcott, a Devonshire, England maid who claimed that she was the first messenger referred to in Revelation 5:1–2:

> *Then I saw the right hand of him who sat on the throne a scroll with writing on both sides and sealed with seven seals.*
> *And I saw a mighty angel proclaiming in a loud voice, "Who is worthy to break the seals and open the scroll?"*

At age sixty-four, Joanna said that she was pregnant with the Seventh Messenger. Doctors confirmed her pregnancy, but Joanna miscarried the child. The House of David recognized Joanna Southcott as the First Messenger. That does raise a logical question: how could the First Messenger be pregnant with the Seventh? Five more English messengers followed: Richard Brothers, George Turner, William Shaw, John Wroe and James Jershom Jazreel.

Purnell claimed that a dove perched on his shoulder and informed him of his destiny. You just can't depend on a dove to get the facts right. Apparently, this one got it wrong and told him that he was only the Sixth Messenger. Purnell later corrected that notion by announcing that he was, in fact, the Seventh Messenger. In his words, "I am the messenger and fire and brimstone await those who doubt me."

He was a seventh son of a seventh son and believed that this confirmed his claim of religious eminence. Members were to come to him and yield all their worldly possessions. There would later be a gathering of the Twelve Tribes of Israel. Benjamin Purnell was the Shiloh.

They first worked as itinerant preachers of the word and settled for a time in Ohio. Two of their early followers helped them in the selection of Benton Harbor, Michigan, as the ideal spot to launch the Israelite House of David. In 1904, the Purnells received a cablegram from Melbourne, Australia, from a sect calling itself the Christian Israelite Church. The church said that it accepted Benjamin Purnell as the Seventh Messenger. Benjamin and Mary immediately traveled to Melbourne and returned with eighty-five new members. It was a fortuitous move because many of the newcomers had skills needed in Benton Harbor.

To give credit where credit is due, what they created there was amazing, especially in light of the fact that both had grown up relatively poor in families where each was one of twelve children. Without formal education and no management or any other marketable experience, Mary and Benjamin Purnell created a communal living situation for the membership, complete with spacious accommodations in luxurious buildings.

Most communes and religious sects keep to themselves and discourage outside scrutiny. The House of David was the complete opposite. In the commune's early days, curiosity seekers came to the grounds to see what was going on. Instead of erecting fences, posting "NO TRESPASSING" signs and employing guards, Benjamin wisely saw people's natural curiosity as a means of making money. Members welcomed visitors and used hospitality to fund the commune.

The resort they named Eden Springs offered amusement park rides, a train, shops, a zoo and dining establishments, and expertly maintained gardens were scattered between the attractions. They were locally famous for their home-churned ice cream in home-baked waffle cones. Benton Harbor residents often visited Eden Springs simply to indulge in the treat. And although the membership eschewed alcohol, the Purnells knew better than to force their clientele to do likewise. Thus, a beer tent was another popular attraction.

Homegrown talent performing live included a girls' band, an orchestra and various musicians. Outsiders were invited to perform in a talent show held weekly. The quality, of course, varied from week to week, leading one attendee to remark that on most of those nights, the "talent" had a much better time than the audiences forced to sit through those weekly entertainments.

The residential buildings were given lofty names that fitted their architectural grandeur. The earlier three were called Bethlehem, Jerusalem and Shiloh, with Shiloh being the most ornate. Each new resident was required to turn all his or her earthly treasure over to the sect. Not all had any treasure to give, and those gave their talents instead. It should be noted here that anyone not having cash or a marketable skill might be encouraged to seek spiritual guidance elsewhere.

What Purnell did excel in was recognizing the potential of each resident, starting with the architect William Wright, one of the Australians, who designed the living quarters. He encouraged one and all to accomplishments far beyond their normal scope. Eden Park and all its attractions, right down to the train, were dreamed, designed and delivered by sect members. And Purnell had the good sense not to micromanage their work. "Give them confidence in their abilities, then sit back and wait for the results" seemed to be his modus operandi, and for him, it worked. Almost without fail. Members built the popular train on which visitors to the park could ride, and they laid the track and even built the steam engine.

At one time, more than one thousand members lived on the property. They were best known for their baseball teams, which barnstormed the country playing exhibition games with pro teams and against the Negro League teams. Satchel Paige played on one of those teams and referred to the Davids, as they were sometimes called, as the Jesus Boys. The men all had long flowing hair and beards. Like basketball's Harlem Globetrotters, they were equal parts athletes and showmen. The House of David teams seldom lost and brought a carnival air to the small towns where they played. Sometimes local schools and some of the businesses closed for the

The steam engine train was designed and built by residents of the Israelite House of David commune. *Detroit Public Library.*

games, a practice that took away the temptation of truancy or calling in sick at work. Baseball was Purnell's way of focusing the celibate players' attention away from sex.

When they couldn't recruit enough good players at home, they hired pros. Dizzy Dean and his brother Daffy played for them, as did Grover Cleveland Alexander, Satchel Paige, Babe Didrikson Zaharias and a seventeen-year-old girl named Jackie Mitchell, who held the distinction of having once struck out Babe Ruth and Lou Gehrig in the same inning during an exhibition game! The men were gracious and even posed for a photograph with young Jackie. Ruth did later say that, in his opinion, women shouldn't play the game, as it was too strenuous.

The biggest problem with the Israelite House of David and other cults is that their structure is that of a pyramid, with the leader firmly entrenched at the top. The *Chicago Tribune* reported in 1910 that witnesses at a street fair told authorities that Purnell slept inside the girls' tent and that the girls were required to dance for him wearing only their nighties.

Many people made it a point to refer to the couple as King Benjamin and Queen Mary. In their defense, they never encouraged that, and in truth, they preferred to be called Brother and Sister.

Although it was usually a man, women have been known to lead these outsider groups. There is a reason these sects are always outside (often way outside!) the mainstream denominations. A scoundrel can't wake up one morning and claim that he had a vision, even if he supports the claim with bogus proof, that he is the rightful pope. If he did, he would soon find himself residing in a mental hospital swapping visions with a motley crew of Abraham Lincolns, Robin Hoods and Queen Victorias.

Scandal threatened the sect when more than a dozen teenage girls accused him of sexually molesting them. He had told them that it was a necessary step in their purification, although he never elaborated on exactly what was impure about the young girls. The *New York Times* reported that Purnell was so ill that he had to carried into the court on a stretcher so he could make his bail. He was then transported by ambulance back to his rooms at Shiloh.

Benjamin was tried and convicted but died of tuberculosis before he could be sentenced. In keeping with their belief that the body doesn't die, his body remained unmoved for three days. Christ may have risen on the third day, but Benjamin Purnell remained immobile.

When it became obvious that he had no intention of ever getting up and walking away, they did the decent thing and embalmed him. But they didn't follow that with a proper burial and chose instead to enshrine him a glass coffin. Someone joked that they placed a hammer in the coffin so he could break the glass if he ever did wake up. To their credit, the coffin was never put on display like a ghoulish museum piece. They stashed it away in a room hidden deep inside the elaborate residence's interior, where it no doubt startled anyone who unknowingly happened upon it.

Following Benjamin's death, the group split into two factions. Mary claimed that she, not Benjamin, was in fact the real Seventh Messenger and seized control of one of them. She changed the name to Mary's City of David. The other members lined up under the leadership of Tom Dewhirst. Mary kept the best baseball team, while Dewhirst, not to be outdone, beefed up the second string.

PREYING ON THE VULNERABLE

Any physician who advertises a positive cure for any disease, who issues nostrum testimonials, who sells his services to a secret remedy, or who diagnoses and treats by mail patients he has never seen is a quack.
—Samuel Hopkins Adams

It seems cruel in the extreme to prey on suffering people by offering a cure that the seller knows for a fact won't do a bit of good. It's especially shameful when that person is a doctor who should know better. The Hippocratic Oath states "do no harm"—not do no harm unless it will substantially line your pockets.

Patent medicine makers hawked their wares across the country, and Michigan was no exception. Traveling medicine shows were frequent events, and although they offered some entertainment, their main purpose was to make readily available a potion or a pill to cure every ailment known to man and, in so doing, separate audience members from their money. Sometimes it was the same remedy packaged under a different name with a new label announcing the cure of a different malady. They often planted shills in the audience to tell the people that the offering of the day had actually snatched them from the jaws of death. Worse, someone might experience a miraculous cure right there in front of everyone.

The venerable Dr. John Harvey Kellogg is included here as he was, in retrospect, half healer and half quack. In some ways, he was ahead of the curve in promoting healthy eating habits, fresh air, exercise and other

James S. and Ellen G. White brought the Seventh-day Adventist denomination to Battle Creek. *Wikimedia Commons*.

Dr. John Harvey Kellogg, founder of the Battle Creek Sanitarium, was part scoundrel and part doctor. *Library of Congress.*

ideas now embraced by modern medicine. Yogurt enemas, not so much. He believed 100 percent in what he called biologic living and was a strict vegetarian. He had been raised in the Seventh-day Adventist denomination founded in Battle Creek by James and Ellen White. The Whites were impressed with his intelligence and mentored him when he decided to become a doctor.

What exactly is "biologic living"? As Dr. Kellogg wrote in 1875 in *The Battle Creek Idea*, the magazine he published:

> *THE HYGIENIC PLATFORM*
> *Obedience to the laws of life and health is a moral obligation.*
> *Mental, moral, and physical health can only be maintained by the observance of mental, moral, and physical laws.*
> *A healthy body is essential to perfect soundness of mind.*
> *Physical health promotes morality.*
> *Morality, likewise promotes physical health.*
> *In the treatment of disease the simplest and safest remedies are the proper curative agents.*
> *Nature is the most efficient physician.*

Not everyone agreed with those ideas. In 1886, the Calhoun County Medical Board sued Kellogg for "promoting ideas unbecoming to a regular physician." The trial ended with a hung jury, and the charges were dropped. The Michigan Medical Board sued on the same charges in 1887 but dropped the charges before the case could be tried. The reason was not made public.

Kellogg received his formal medical education at the Bellevue Hospital Medical College in New York. Upon his return to Battle Creek, the Whites hired him to run the Sanitarium, the Seventh-day Adventist hospital/spa/resort/medical training facility known nationwide as the San. Founded in 1866 and originally called the Western Reform Health Institute, it was the largest facility of its kind in the country and at its peak could accommodate about 1,300 guests.

It was Kellogg who renamed it the Sanitarium. When he was told that there was no such word, he said people would intuitively know it was a place where they could learn to be healthy, unlike a hospital, where they would go to be cured. Kellogg ran the San from 1876 to 1943.

People flocked to the San to fine-tune their health. Famous clientele included Henry Ford, Presidents Warren G. Harding and William Howard Taft, Amelia Earhart, J.C. Penney and even Mary Todd Lincoln on at least one occasion.

Guests being treated at the San found their days filled with exercises, hydrotherapy, yogurt enemas, lectures and medical consultations. Even mealtimes were occasions for more San propaganda. One edict was that each mouthful should be chewed at least forty times. Often Dr. Kellogg himself led diners in raising their voices in a rousing chorus of the "Chewing Song":

Chew, chew, chew
that is the thing to do
you may smile when you do
but don't try to talk too
for perhaps you will choke
and be sorry you spoke

There were more verses, many more, but like this one they are best forgotten. Somehow, it's hard to imagine former presidents and Mary Todd Lincoln belting out the "Chewing Song."

John Harvey blamed many diseases on the bowels and accordingly treated patients with frequent, often daily, yogurt enemas. The role of the bowels in all-around health might not have been too big a stretch for the doctor, as he had suffered from constipation his whole childhood.

He further believed that any disease that couldn't be blamed on the lack of proper bowel movements was caused by sex. So, in his opinion, the only way to maintain good health was total abstinence. He probably found few who would agree. Fortunately for him, his wife, Ella Eaton Kellogg, was one of those few—he practiced what he preached and never consummated his own marriage. All seven of the couple's children were adopted.

Sex was another of the many issues on which the Kellogg brothers disagreed. Will Keith married Ella Davis in 1880 and, following her death, married Carrie Staines in 1918. He consummated his marriages, resulting in five children: Will Keith Jr., Karl Hugh, Elizabeth Ann, John Leonard and Ann Janette. He outlived all but two, Elizabeth Ann and Karl Hugh.

In John Harvey's view, the most heinous sin was masturbation. As he put it, "Many mothers are wholly ignorant of the almost universal prevalence of secret vice, or self-abuse, among the young. Why hesitate to say firmly and without quibble that personal abuse lies at the root of much of the feebleness, paleness, nervousness, and good-for-nothingness of the entire community?" Finally, a valid explanation for those good-for-nothings!

He treated male sinners by performing circumcisions without benefit of anesthesia, partly as punishment but also so the offender would associate pain with that part of his anatomy. Girls who engaged in that wicked behavior received carbolic acid treatments aimed at the clitoris, a practice that sounds too painful to even think about.

Only five-foot-four, with a slender build, Kellogg made up for his stature with an outsized flamboyance. He usually dressed all in white: suit, shirt, tie and shoes. This was his year-round wardrobe, and as white is notoriously hard to keep clean, he changed his suit at least once during each day. He must have looked like an apparition to patients just waking up from anesthesia. Dr. Kellogg complemented his fantastical appearance with theatrical behavior.

He became friends with Drs. William and Charles Mayo, who with their father, William Moran Mayo, founded the renowned Mayo Clinic in Rochester, Minnesota. He even visited the facility, but as impressed as he was, he never seriously considered bringing the best of the best in all medical specialties to the San. His oversized ego could never permit him to share the spotlight with other doctors. All San surgeries were performed by Dr. Kellogg alone.

Dr. Kellogg recruited his younger brother to be his general gofer. Will Keith co-managed the San and took care of the business end of the enterprise. He also served as John Harvey's personal secretary and was treated abominably. The doctor was known to make his secretary pedal along beside him on a bicycle to take dictation. The situation continued until Will Keith left the San entirely to run the cereal company.

At some point, Kellogg began questioning some of the church's practices, at least as far as they applied to medicine. The church expelled him in 1906. Will Keith was also expelled but took it philosophically. "Since I haven't attended church in 27 years, I can't really blame them," he said. John Harvey never joined another church. A friend compared him to Abraham Lincoln, who preferred being independent of any established creed or sect.

Dr. Kellogg manufactured and sold his own concoction to keep men virile well into their seventies. It's not known exactly how he defined virile, but one definition is in direct conflict with his views on sex. He also developed a belt-like device to be worn by men to keep them from touching themselves in a way that would result in masturbation. It's unknown if he was able to persuade any men to wear it.

The most disturbing of his interests came with his three-decade study of eugenics and his resulting belief that the human race could be bettered through selective breeding. This, of course, included the sterilization of specimens of mankind deemed inferior. At the other end of the spectrum, reproduction would be arranged among those exhibiting desirable traits. In 1914, he hosted the First National Conference on Race Betterment at the San. Sounds like a good idea, but only for those who breed racehorses or show dogs.

One early proponent of this was Sir Francis Galton, but the idea became discredited as unscientific and racist in the early to mid-twentieth century. That's when Adolf Hitler appeared on the scene and exposed the idea's most horrific potential in the Nazis' treatment of Jews, the disabled and other minorities. Dr. Kellogg died in 1943, so he never saw the appalling outcome of such a philosophy.

It wasn't all bogus. John Harvey's brother and business partner, William Keith Kellogg, manufactured and sold what eventually came to be called corn flakes, but it happened due to an error. He (or John Harvey) became distracted while baking a batch of something and forgot to take it out of the oven. When someone finally removed the concoction, it had flaked nicely. The brothers disagreed over this and pretty much everything else. John Harvey wanted to keep it exclusively for the San clientele, while William Keith thought that it should be available to the masses. Fortunately, William Keith prevailed, and cold cereal became a breakfast staple. How could our kids exist without Froot Loops?

W. K. KELLOGG 1860-1951

Will Keith Kellogg, brother of John Harvey and the man behind the cereal empire. *Library of Congress.*

The brothers' contempt for each other was no secret, partly due to occasional lawsuits they filed against each other. They were sometimes referred to as Battle Creek's Cain and Abel. The tensions between the brothers were further complicated by the fact that Dr. Kellogg's wife, Ella, thoroughly disliked William Keith and wasn't above giving her husband exaggerated reports of what she considered errors on his part. In the end, John Harvey is almost forgotten. William Keith's sound business practices and personal integrity led to today's Kellogg's company and is known and respected around the world. His initials still appear on every box of Kellogg's brand cereal.

In 1930, he established the W.K. Kellogg Foundation for the purpose of administering funds for the promotion of the welfare, comfort, health, educating, feeding, clothing, sheltering and safeguarding of children and youth, directly or indirectly, without regard to sex, race, creed or nationality. He instructed the original and future trustees and staff to "[u]se the money as you please so long as it promotes the health, happiness, and well-being of children." Today, it is recognized as one of the world's largest private foundations awarding grants in the United States, Mexico and Haiti. The Grand Rapids and Kalamazoo public television station is one of the recipients of the foundation's philanthropy.

Dr. John Kellogg was not Battle Creek's only medical fraudster. Dr. Samuel Peeble was another genuine doctor who should have known better. His Battle Creek Institute of Health's main claim to fame was a phony cure for epileptic seizures. It was later discovered that the treatment sometimes caused homicidal tendencies. Maybe those pesky seizures weren't so bad after all.

William Keith Kellogg's cereal competitor, Charles W. Post, who preferred to be called C.W., spent about nine months at the San, inviting the question: Was he there as a guest or as a corporate spy? Whatever he did there, he later opened his own short-lived competing spa, La Vita Inn. Post's spa had one ironclad rule: no medicines—ever.

The La Vita Inn was established to offer guests the exact opposite of what they would receive at the vegetarian San. Post offered steak and bacon in large quantities. Also, "no dieting or water therapy treatments, graham bread, bran mush, and various forms of nonsense that often go under the name of hygiene."

Also, while at the San, Post observed cereal being made, and Post, not Kellogg, was the first to sell dry cereal to the public. Post also introduced a cereal-based coffee substitute he named Postum, which initially enjoyed wide distribution, but at its most popular, it never really posed a threat to a real cup of joe.

He makes the quack list because he claimed that his company's Grape Nuts cereal would cure appendicitis. Ironically, he suffered frequent abdominal pain that he blamed on his appendix. He reportedly even went to the Mayo Clinic for relief, an act that proved he didn't quite believe his own claim of the curative powers to be found in a large bowl of Grape Nuts.

He was fined $50,000 for this false claim, a hefty sum that today would be almost $1.5 million. Post committed suicide on May 19, 1914, one reason being his chronic pain. His daughter Marjorie Merriweather Post, with her husband, E.F. Hutton, took over the company and shaped it into what eventually became General Foods.

In 1993, T.C. Boyle published a novel spoofing Dr. Kellogg, *The Road to Wellville*, but it was Post, not Kellogg, who coined the term to describe his own spa.

Battle Creek is today called Cereal City and not just because of Kellogg and Post. About one hundred cereal companies popped up in Battle Creek over the years, but most failed almost immediately.

Marshall was home to more patent medicine sellers than any other town in the state. *Wikimedia Commons.*

Marshall claimed the most and was given the dubious honor of becoming known as Medicine City. But many other towns across the state also produced patent medicines with little or no medicinal value. Hinckley's Bone Liniment was made in Saginaw. H.D. Cushman of Three Rivers produced Cushman's Menthol Inhaler, advertised as a cure for diseases of the head, including hay fever, colds and bronchitis.

Grand Rapids had a self-proclaimed urine inspector, a Dr. VanWesterveld, who proved his quack status when someone sent him three separate vials of exactly the same liquid and received three separate diagnoses. The vials presented for inspection contained a variety of fluids, but notably, not even a single drop of urine was present in any of them.

Coca-Cola was developed in May 1886 by an Atlanta, Georgia pharmacist, Dr. John Pemberton, who first used the syrup as a patent medicine. The name came from two of the ingredients, cola leaves and African kola nuts, which provided the caffeine. He claimed that his new concoction could cure indigestion, headaches, morphine addiction and even impotence.

It was a natural progression to add carbonated water to the syrup and create the soft drink, which was first served in Atlanta drugstore soda fountains. Unlike the original product, today's Coke no longer contains cocaine, a drug legal at the time and commonly used in medicines. And it no longer is claimed to cure a laundry list of medical conditions.

Lydia Pinkham's Vegetable Compound was first introduced in 1875 for the treatment and cure of "female complaints" and is still used today. The original formula contained herbs, life root, black cohosh, unicorn root, fenugreek root, pleurisy root and that long-favored miracle ingredient of most patent medicines: alcohol.

Pinkham claimed that her product energized the uterus, thus reducing the chance of miscarriage, enhance the likelihood of conception, lessen the pain of menstruation and ease hot flashes and other symptoms of menopause. The alcohol and any other potentially harmful ingredients have been removed, and the current product is only used to ease discomfort.

In June 1906, Congress passed the first FDA law requiring makers of medicines list all alcohol and other addictive ingredients to those ingredients on their packaging, as well as the amount of the substance each dose contained. The act was signed into law by President Theodore Roosevelt. The law effectively put many unscrupulous manufacturers and marketers of potentially harmful products out of business.

Not all the faux cures involved pills or potions. Some, like Mary Eliason of Kalamazoo, believed that electricity had healing powers and called herself a medical electrician. This was long before electric shock treatments were commonly used to treat mental diseases, so this so-called electrician must have had to look long and hard to find people who were brave enough to endure the treatment.

FROM DRAFTSMAN
TO FINANCIAL WIZARD
TO FUGITIVE ON THE RUN

A billion here, a billion there—pretty soon it adds up to some real money.
—Senator Everett Dirksen

Robert Lee Vesco was born in Detroit on December 4, 1935, the son of a Chrysler assembly line worker. He dropped out of high school at sixteen to become an apprentice in an automotive body shop. He later admitted to having had three goals in those days: get the hell out of Detroit, become president of a corporation and be a millionaire by age thirty. Rather lofty goals for a dropout, but a lack of a formal education would not be a problem, as there are no known colleges that offer majors in swindling.

He changed jobs a few times and eventually went to work as a draftsman in the Reynolds Metals Company Detroit sales office. He soon found that a bit too boring, not to mention relatively low-paying; at least it seemed that way to someone of his lofty visions. Vesco knew that he could exponentially increase his income by working in finance.

He soon was doing so well that he was called the boy wonder of international finance. At the top of his game, he could have rivaled the fictional "greed is good" Gordon Gekko. He conned and/or corrupted various heads of state around the world.

By age thirty, had gained millionaire status and also gained control of a small automotive machine company, renaming it International Controls

Corporation. Over the next five years, he took advantage of ICC's rising stock price fueled by a bull market and dubious accounting to borrow additional sums of money, which he used to take ICC on a buying spree, further boosting its stock price. In just three years, he took his company's annual sales from $1.3 million to more than $100 million.

In January 1971, he took control of the Swiss-based Investor Overseas Services then managed by Bernard Cornfield, which sold and ran various "funds of funds" funds that were used to invest in other funds. Although he claimed he acquired the IOS to clean up the fraudulent practices of Cornfield, in reality he increased the swindling.

Vesco emerged as a key figure in several financial and political scandals in the early '70s. The U.S. Securities and Exchange Commission accused him and his associates of looting the IOS of $224 million, thereby defrauding thousands of investors by diverting assets from mutual funds. In 1976, he was indicted by a federal grand jury on IOS fraudulent schemes.

Forced to flee the United States in 1972, he spent various periods of time living a life of luxury in Costa Rica, the Bahamas, Nicaragua and Antigua. During one of his Antigua stays, he tried to buy its island Barbuda so he could set it up as a sovereign state. The deal never happened, but it wasn't because Vesco lacked the funds. In each country, he allegedly employed political bribery, and none granted extradition requests from the United States and Switzerland, where IOS was headquartered.

His public relations man said that Vesco did not want to be a Howard Hughes and did not want to hide from anyone. Maybe not, but he obviously didn't want to be found either. His skill in talking out of both sides of his mouth would have served him well had he decided to go into politics. That was something he probably never seriously considered, as politicians then didn't amass the kind of wealth that Vesco did.

Vesco accomplished his political maneuvers in the shadows. In 1980, he was reported to have persuaded the Libyan government to pay President Jimmy Carter's brother, Billy, $220,000 as part of an oil deal that never happened. Billy Carter, of course, is best remembered as the inspiration behind the short-lived Billy Beer. Billy is probably the sibling who pushed Mama Lillian into saying, "Sometimes I look at my children and say, Lillian, you should have stayed a virgin."

Vesco's time in Nicaragua came during the period the Sandinistas were in power. That country, like the others where he found protection, welcomed him with open arms, as they knew of his immense wealth. It would be hard not to, as his name was a regular on the *Forbes* list of the world's four hundred wealthiest people. His occupation was listed as "thief." Obviously, they hoped some of that seemingly inexhaustible stream of cash would find its way into some of the local development projects. It probably never did, as philanthropy is not something for which Robert Vesco is remembered.

While abroad, he increased his stolen wealth through further large investments, notably in international arms sales to Libya, among other countries, and drug trafficking with a Colombian cartel.

In the early 1980s, he went to Cuba, where he had more than one home, a private airplane and a yacht. Somewhere along the way, he married a Cuban woman, Lidia Alphonso Liariga. He was arrested in Cuba in 1996 for a few economic crimes he committed there. Lidia was also arrested and charged. She was convicted of lesser offenses and received a lighter sentence. One of Vesco's crimes consisted of conning a biotech company owned by a nephew of President Fidel Castro. He convinced the owner that he could develop and produce a new wonder drug. Castro refused to extradite him to the United States. After serving a thirteen-year sentence, he was released from a Cuban jail in 2005.

Vesco is believed to have died of lung cancer on November 23, 2007, in Havana, Cuba, after amassing a lifetime total of more than $200 million through fraud. Still, there are some who say that it could have been later, or not at all, and that he could be alive and well in a country without an extradition agreement with the United States.

One of his close associates, Frank Tepil, insisted that Vesco was still alive and had fled to Sierra Leone. An episode of the television series *Blacklist* features a fictionalized version of him in the sixth season; in that show, Vesco does indeed fake his own death.

His death was reported by Reuters, the *New York Times* and other leading media heavyweights. And it was verified by a relative who has remained anonymous and who claimed to have attended the funeral. The records of Havana's Colon Cemetery do show that a Robert Lee Vesco was buried there in November 2007 in a tomb belonging to a family named Rives.

"We don't know where the money is but I can assure you that he is dead because I attended the funeral," said the relative, who reportedly lives in a squalid Havana apartment. It sounds credible, but it wouldn't be the first funeral held without a corpse in attendance. How hard would it be for someone with the intelligence required to steal $200 million? On the off chance that he is still alive, he would be eighty-eight in 2023, so he would likely be retired—if people in that line of work retire.

As far as the money is concerned, there probably would have been little, if any, left at the time of his death. His lavish lifestyle, along with the necessity of distributing bribes to pay for his protection from extradition, would have made a sizeable dent in his bank balance.

ORGANIZED CRIME IN MICHIGAN

*It's no secret that organized crime in America takes in over $40 billion a year.
This is quite a profitable sum, especially when one considers that the Mafia
spends very little on office supplies.*
—Woody Allen

THE PURPLE GANG

The gang was made up of the offspring of Jewish immigrants who came first to New York between 1881 and 1914, mostly from Poland and Russia. Eventually, they made their way to Detroit. Four brothers—Abe, Joe, Raymond and Izzy Bernstein—led the group of outlaws that was known for its excessive use of violence. They are the country's only Jewish gang to prey on one of America's major cities, thus earning the nickname the "Kosher Nostra."

Except for the Detroit mafia, Michigan's greatest contribution to organized crime was the Purple Gang, sometimes called the Sugar House Gang. Some say they got their name because one of the leaders was a boxer who wore purple shorts during his contests. Another, more likely, explanation comes from an alleged conversation between two shopkeepers when the gangsters were still children: "These boys are not like other children of their age. They are tainted. Off color," said the first.

"Yes," the second replied. "They're rotten, purple like the color of spoiled meat. They are a purple gang."

However they came by the name, they were a Detroit-based gang of Jewish thugs who began their chicanery while still boys and reigned supreme from 1910 to the 1930s. The peak of their power came during the Prohibition era in the 1920s. The Purple Gang pretty much controlled all the bootleg whiskey coming into the state from Canada via the Detroit River and later the Detroit Windsor Tunnel, sometimes referred to as the Detroit Windsor Funnel. They were known for their brutality and are believed to have killed more than five hundred rivals.

One of their rivals was Joseph Kennedy, father of John, Bobby and Ted Kennedy. The elder Kennedy was bootlegging whiskey from Ireland and England and brought it from Canada via the Detroit River. He probably never knew that to do so required the permission of the bloodthirsty Purples, nor was he accustomed to asking permission for anything he chose to do. The Purples arranged for a contract killing. Kennedy had friends who were higher up in the criminal hierarchy and called in a favor from Chicago's Joseph "Diamond Joe" Esposito, who managed to have the death threat canceled.

At one time, Detroit claimed more than twenty-five thousand speakeasies. The Purples controlled most of them and other criminal activity in Detroit as well. That included horse racing, other gambling, prostitution, money-laundering, fencing and the drug trade. They acquired some of their liquor inventory by stopping vessels on the river, stealing the goods at gunpoint and killing the drivers. They could not be written off as local gangsters who had gotten too big for their britches because they had powerful underworld allies, including Meyer Lansky and Joe Adonis. Lansky and Abe Bernstein together developed the National Crime Syndicate.

The Purples were Al Capone's primary source for ill-gotten booze in Michigan. Capone recognized their power, and rather than engage in a turf war, he decided to partner with them. Capone sold his booze in Chicago and once said, "When I sell alcohol, it's called bootlegging. When my Lake Shore Drive clientele serves it, it's called hospitality."

After Prohibition, they became involved in the Cleaners and Dyers War, harassing and bombing all who resisted their extortion demands. After that war ended, nine Purple Gang members were charged with extortion. All nine were guilty but acquitted, making it likely that bribery and jury tampering allowed them to get away with their crimes.

The notorious gang began its downward spiral in part due to infighting. Abe Bernstein invited three members to a peace summit at an apartment on Collingwood Avenue: Herman (Hymie) Paul, Joe Surker and Joseph. All three were gunned down upon arrival, allegedly for betraying the gang.

The Purples all but disappeared from scrutiny in the late 1930s. Incarceration, death and retirements greatly reduced their number, and the few left were absorbed into the Detroit mafia, with one notable exception: Harry Millman.

Millman refused to take orders from the Sicilians and earned a reputation as a loose cannon. It is pretty much common knowledge that mobsters do not tolerate loose cannons in their midst. Add to that he had a short fuse, a penchant for barroom brawling and was an alcoholic, all of which rendered him long on guts but short on brains. This combination made Detroit police detective Harold Branton say, "His number is up, and it's only a matter of time. He has kept himself on the streets with his guns and his fists. He is going to die one of these days and die violently."

Millman found his way back to Detroit after graduating from a Kentucky military academy in the late 1920s. There he hung out at blind pigs and pool halls run by the Purples and eventually became a hijacker and gunman for the gang. The Purples would regret taking him on, as his reputation for violence grew, as did his reputation for brazen actions. He especially liked going into a mafia-protected enterprises like speakeasies, knocking customers off their barstools and then beating up anyone who tried to stop him.

Initially, the Bernstein brothers managed to keep Millman alive, even though mafia thugs met with them for the express purpose of demanding Millman be executed. They would promise to talk some sense into him, but that proved to be an exercise in futility.

The first attempt at killing Millman failed miserably. The bomb planted in his car exploded when a valet named Willie Holmes was driving. The incident is believed to be Detroit's first car bombing.

On November 24, 1937, Millman was gunned down in a restaurant. The ten bullets later removed from his body are said to have killed him before his body ever hit the floor. When the truth came out, it was not only the Detroit mafia that wanted Millman gone. The hit was jointly ordered by the Purples and the Italians.

Although the Purple Gang had largely disappeared by 1940, a few remaining members continued operating independently and had one more murder to commit. As soon as Sam and Harry Fleisher were released from Alcatraz, they set their sights on Warren Hooper. It seems that the Jewish mobsters also enjoyed exacting revenge on real or perceived enemies.

On January 11, 1945, State Senator Warren Hooper was gunned down on Highway M99 while driving from his Lansing office to his home in Albion. After forcing his car off the road, the assassins shot him three times.

This occurred just a few days before Hooper was scheduled to testify before a grand jury about corruption in the state government and implicate more than a few scoundrels who preferred keeping their crimes secret.

One of those was Grand Rapids' self-made millionaire Frank D. McKay, who was suspected of, but never charged with, initiating and funding the hit. He was believed to be the puppet master behind at least two Michigan governors. He dabbled in several industries but was primarily a financier and bought the eighteen-story Grand Rapids National Bank Building located downtown on the corner of Pearl Street and Monroe Center. He immediately renamed it McKay Tower.

State Senator Warren G. Hooper was murdered to prevent his testimony before a grand jury. *Michigan History Center.*

McKay was often referred to as "Boss McKay" but claimed that he had never bossed anyone. As he put it, "Boss is what newspapers call influential men they don't like. If they like you, you're a political leader." Although he was considered a kingmaker, his own political career consisted only of being elected state treasurer three times. He left office under accusations of cronyism and misuse of state funds.

Although he was suspected of various criminal acts, he avoided being prosecuted and was thought to have threatened, bribed or, in Hooper's case, murdered those who thought they could bring him down. An honest politician was something of a rarity at that time in Michigan history, and he paid the ultimate price. His tombstone reads, "With honesty he lived. For honesty he was taken." The murder remains officially unsolved, although Purple Ganger Sam Abramowitz said that he, Mike Selik and Pete Mahoney had been hired by Harry Fleisher to do the deed.

THE DETROIT MAFIA

The Detroit version of the Italian mafioso made one of its first appearances in Michigan in the early days of the twentieth century with the murder of three area brothers: Gaetano, Antonio (Tony) and Salvatore (Sam) Gianola, who owned and operated a small grocery and fruit market. In 1911, the police received a tip, allegedly from Sam Benudo, who had formerly been an associate of the Gianolas. Benudo strongly suggested that the authorities should check out a charred body that was found in a field. It appeared that someone had exacted revenge on behalf of the fallen Gianola brothers.

One thing to remember about the Detroit mafia is that they seemed to be a bigger threat to one another than to the good people of Detroit in general. The various "families" were usually at war.

If ever a law was made to encourage the growth of organized crime, Prohibition was it. While the Volstead Act brought organized crime to the forefront, the mobs were actually involved in bootlegging back before it became illegal. The goal was to bring in booze from Canada to Michigan at low cost so as to sell it for less than the legitimate distillers. After the Eighteenth Amendment became law, the object became just taking it out of Canada and bringing it into Michigan.

About 75 percent of all the illegal alcohol entering the United States flowed from Windsor, Canada, into Michigan via the Detroit River. It quickly became Detroit's second-largest industry, outdone only by the automotive giants.

Rumrunning may have been a profitable business, but it was also a violent one. In the early years of Prohibition, between 1919 and 1923, the various law enforcement agencies blamed nearly 100 homicides on the alcohol trade. Some of those were attributed to the Detroit mafia killing independent rival bootleggers. Others were suspected of being done by non-Italian gangs, including the Jewish Purple Gang, the Legs Lamon and the Little Jewish Navy. In 1927–28, Detroit police shot and killed 70 people and wounded more than 130 more. By the end of the next year, federal agents had killed another 44 in Detroit Prohibition-related confrontations.

The secret crime organization has been called various names over the years, including the Detroit Mafia, the Detroit Partnership, the Detroit Crime Family, the Zerilli Crime Family and the Tocco Zerilli Crime Family. Call it what you will, by any name it was and is a vicious organized crime group with Sicilian roots.

Mafia-based crime rose exponentially in Detroit and everywhere else during the Prohibition era, and several separate groups existed in the east side of Detroit and Grosse Pointe; in the west side and Dearborn; in Hamtramck, a separate city completely surrounded by Detroit; and downriver in Wyandotte.

The mafia is still alive and well both in Detroit and around the world, although rumrunning is no longer its primary focus. Today's Detroit Partnership, as it's called, has its fingers in a mind-boggling number of pies:

illegal gambling, including sports betting; money laundering; racketeering; police corruption; narcotics trafficking; smuggling; loan sharking; fraud; and, when called for, murder. How did they ever find time for bootlegging?

The Detroit mob is suspected to be responsible for Jimmy Hoffa's disappearance, as two of its key figures were who he supposedly was meeting with; most, if not all, of the key players are dead.

Al Capone

Alphonse Capone was the first member of his birth family to be born in the United States. His older siblings were born in Italy, while he and the younger Capones were born in Brooklyn. While still a child, he proved himself as someone who could be trusted by the New York criminal element. The Chicagoland gangster was no stranger in Michigan, as he maintained a residence in the southwestern part of the state in and around the Berrien area, but most of the Capone-induced bloodshed happened back in Illinois. Even the worst of the worst needed a place to chill out and regroup in between murders and general sprees of mayhem. He laid low for the most part and was even considered a good neighbor.

Capone viewed himself not as a monster, but as a businessman. "I'm no angel. I've had to do things I didn't want to do," he once said. "But I'm human and I have a heart in me." He did, and his generosity is well documented. On the other hand, so is his brutality.

Because there were times when he needed more than a place to relax, Capone also had a pad he used as a hideaway in Lansing. Residents later recalled seeing parades of black Cadillacs and Lincolns heading for the property. Not knowing whether it was their neighbor himself and his entourage or another criminal gang coming to do him harm, they played it safe and stayed in. They further instructed their children to stay in and refrain from standing in front of any windows. At a sudden, unexpected noise, whole families would hit the floor.

"Do not mistake my kindness for weakness. I am kind to everyone, but if you are unkind to me, it will not be kindness that you will remember me for," he once said. It should be noted that he considered it an unkindness in the extreme to be called "Scarface," so no one in his inner circle ever used that nickname, at least not to his scarred face. Contrary to popular opinion, he did not receive the scars from another mobster. They came during a bar fight over a woman.

A fake Al Capone on display in Berrien Springs reminds us of the time the gangster spent in the area. *Library of Congress.*

At age eighteen, Capone had a job working as a bouncer at the Harvard Inn at Coney Island. One night, a young thug named Frank Gallucio came in with two girls: his date, Maria Tanzo, and his sister, Lena. Capone found Lena attractive and invited her to walk on the beach with him. She said no, and a little later he asked her again, that time adding, "I'll tell you one thing, you got a nice ass."

She told her brother, who demanded Capone apologize. He refused, saying that he was only kidding around. Gallucio was a lot smaller than Capone, so instead of trying to fight him, he grabbed a knife and slashed him three times. The injuries required eighty stitches. Frankie Vale later intervened and made Gallucio give Capone $1,500. He also made Capone promise never to retaliate.

After later serving seven years in prison, Al Capone died at his home in Miami, Florida, on January 25, 1947. Anyone feeling sympathy for him because of his incarceration should note that while the walls were shabby, his cell was more elegantly furnished than many law-abiding citizens' homes. He was forty-eight but had long suffered from syphilis and was so ravaged by the disease that he was said have had the mind of a twelve-year-old in the last months of his life. He was tenderly taken care of by his beloved wife, Mae, who lived quietly for another fifty years.

Capone bristled at being referred to as Italian. Anyone who did so was quickly reminded that he was a proud American, born and bred in Brooklyn, New York, not a half a world away in Sicily.

Baby Face Nelson

This desperado answered to other names over the years, but Baby Face Nelson is the one by which he was best known. He went down in history as one of the best of the best in the bank robbing business, but he was no instant success. In fact, his first attempt happened in Grand Haven, Michigan, where he made a laughable mess of it.

First of all, the teller he approached stepped on a pedal that sounded the alarm not only at the police station but also at the furniture store next door. The store owner grabbed a gun and ran toward the bank. The getaway driver saw the gun-totin' would-be superhero and quickly made the decision to get away while he still could.

The robbers emerged from the bank and, uh-oh, no getaway driver. The police had also arrived on the scene, and both sides fired shots. Some of the buildings suffered wounds, but only one person was hit, suffering only a superficial injury. The desperados had only one option: steal a car. They messed that up too and ended up stealing three. One blew a tire, and another almost immediately ran out of gas. Anybody can have one of those days where they can't do anything right—even bank robbers have them.

Newspapers had a field day with "getaway car that got away" stories, but thugs are notoriously lacking when it comes to a sense of humor, so Nelson and his cohorts likely saw only public humiliation in the situation. The moral in that story is that if you're going to be scared into running out on a gang of bank robbers, it's probably best to run away on foot and leave the car where they can easily find it. Nelson's getaway driver was later gunned down in Chicago.

Baby Face became very good at robbing banks and robbed his way all the way to the top of the Most Wanted List. But he never returned to Grand Haven to do the job right. It might have been because he was too embarrassed.

SELECTED BIBLIOGRAPHY

Bernstein, Arnie. *Bath Massacre: America's First School Bombing*. Ann Arbor: University of Michigan Press, 2009.

Bidwell, Austin Biron. *Bidwell's Travels: From Wall Street to London Prison*. N.p.: Lector House, LLP, 2021.

Booth, Nicolas. *The Thieves of Threadneedle Street: The Incredible True Story of the American Forgers Who Nearly Broke the Bank of England*. N.p., 2016.

Henry, E. William. *Fatal Alliance: The Prosecution, Imprisonment, and Gangland Murder of Jimmy Hoffa*. Andover, MA: Andover Press, 2012.

Kavoeff, Paul R. *The Purple Gang: Organized Crime in Detroit, 1910–1946*. Fort Lee, NJ: Barricade Books, 2000.

Lehto, Steve. *Death's Door: The Truth Behind Michigan's Largest Mass Murder*. Troy, MI: Momentum Books, 2006.

Link, Mardi. *When Evil Came to Good Hart: An Up North Michigan Cold Case*. Ann Arbor: University of Michigan Press, 2006.

Markel, Howard. *The Kelloggs: The Battling Brothers of Battle Creek*. New York: Pantheon Books, 2017.

Moldea, Dan E. *The Hoffa Wars: The Rise and Fall of Jimmy Hoffa*. New York: Open Road Media, 2021.

Shephard, Charles E. *Forgiven: The Rise and Fall of Jim Bakker and the PTL Ministry*. New York: Atlantic Monthly Press, 1989.

Sloane, Arthur A. *Hoffa*. Cambridge: Massachusetts Institute of Technology, 1991.

Stanton, Tom. *Terror in the City of Champions: Murder, Baseball and the Secret Society that Shocked Depression-Era Detroit*. Gilford, CT: LP Books, imprint of Bowman and Littlefield, 2017.

Thompson, Mark. *Molitor: The Murder of a Northern Michigan King*. Presque Isle, MI: Presque Isle Historical Museum, 2020.

Van Noord, Roger. *Assassination of a Michigan King: The Life of James Jesse Strang*. Ann Arbor: University of Michigan Press, 1997. First published in 1988 as *King of Beaver Island* by the University of Illinois Press.

Wilson, Brian C. *Dr. John Harvey Kellogg and the Religion of Biologic Living*. Bloomington: Indiana University Press, 2014.

Website Sources

American Mafia History. "Detroit (Zerilli) Mob Leaders." www.mafiahistory.us/maf-b-de.html.

Bidwell Museum. www.bidwellmuseum.org.

Internet Archives. "The Black Legion Riders." www.archives.org/stream//TheBlackLegionRiders/BLR_djvu.txt.

Joseph Smith Papers. www.josephsmithpapers.com.

Doctoral Thesis

Trupiano, Teresa Lou. "Patent Medicine Town: A Social History of Patent Medicine in Marshall, Michigan." Western Michigan University, 1985.

INDEX

G

H

I

J

K

L

V

W

Z

ABOUT THE AUTHOR

uthor and historian Norma Lewis lives in Grand Haven, Michigan. Michigan Scoundrels is her tenth book for Arcadia Publishing/ The History Press.

Visit us at
www.historypress.com